WAINWRIGHT'S
COAST TO COAST WALK

Also by A. Wainwright and Derry Brabbs

FELLWALKING WITH WAINWRIGHT
WAINWRIGHT ON THE PENNINE WAY

WAINWRIGHT'S
COAST TO COAST WALK

Photographs by

DERRY BRABBS

GUILD PUBLISHING LONDON

CONTENTS

First published in Great Britain by Michael Joseph Ltd
27 Wrights Lane, London W8 5TZ

This edition published 1987 by Book Club Associates by arrangement
with Michael Joseph.

© Text and new line drawings A. Wainwright 1987
© Photographs Derry Brabbs 1987
© Original line drawings Westmorland Gazette

Typeset by Cambridge Photosetting Services, Cambridge
Printed in Italy by New Inter Litho

St Bees

INTRODUCTION

IN 1967, after my retirement from work, I walked the Pennine Way, which had then recently been opened to the public as a continuous long-distance footpath along the spine of northern England. As befitted my new status as a 'senior citizen', I did the walk in easy stages, a few miles at a time. I was singularly ill-fated in the matter of weather on these forays, often being soaked by sluicing rain, nor did I take kindly to the lengthy stretches of glutinous moorland between the various highlights of the journey. While still maintaining that any sort of walking is better than no walking at all, I cannot truthfully say that I enjoyed the Pennine Way.

But the concept of long-distance walking on established rights of way greatly appealed to me and after much study of maps I decided to plan another route on similar lines but in kinder terrain. First of all, it would have to be in the northern counties of England, with which I was already familiar and personally preferred to other parts of the country. Secondly, I wanted the starting point and finishing point to be exactly defined and not a source of doubt; the obvious choices were the high-tide levels of the two seas bordering the north of England, the Irish Sea and the North Sea.

By laying a ruler across the map, the route almost chose itself: the most spectacular point on the western seaboard was St Bees Head, and in the same latitude on the east coast was the quaint and attractive resort of Robin Hood's Bay. Furthermore, the ruler passed through three National Parks – the Lake District, the Yorkshire Dales and the North York Moors – and three-quarters of the distance lay within the boundaries of these areas of outstanding beauty. And nowhere along this line was there an industrial blemish.

The detail was less easy to determine. Could a route be planned that linked existing rights of way throughout? I collected a set of Ordnance Survey maps and after long study devised a way that led only along permitted paths or areas of open access and avoided trespass on private land. This was it, then. St Bees Head to Robin Hood's Bay.

Many walkers who have now trodden the Coast to Coast Walk have wondered why, when I came to write about it, I preferred a west to east crossing instead of the reverse direction, pointing out that when travelling west to east, the finest scenery, that of the Lake District, comes first and would be better reserved as a grand climax. I still think I was correct in my preference. The route lies on a lateral axis and the natural sequence seems to me to be from left to right, just as in writing a letter or reading the lines of a page or listing the people in a group photograph. Going from right to left along a horizontal plane is abnormal, like working against the grain. This might be a personal idiosyncrasy and have no foundation in logic.

My second reason is more cogent. The prevailing weather, including wind and rain, comes from the west on five days out of six and it is more comfortable to have the elements on the back and not in the face, helping rather than hindering progress. And thirdly, while agreeing that the Lake District is the most beautiful and exciting section, I would certainly not concede that the rest of the journey is in the nature of anti-climax. Indeed, the last stage of the walk over the North York Moors is delightful, a joy to tread, and the first sighting of the North Sea from an upland expanse of heather may well be thought the greatest moment of all.

Robin Hood's Bay

St Bees Head

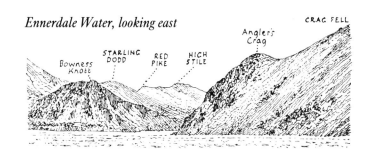
Ennerdale Water, looking east

CRAG FELL

Angler's Crag

Bowness Knott · STARLING DODD · RED PIKE · HIGH STILE

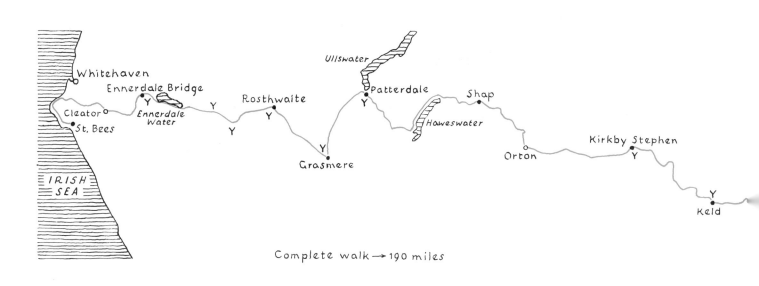

Whitehaven

Ennerdale Bridge

Cleator

St. Bees

IRISH SEA

Ennerdale Water

Y

Y

Rosthwaite

Y

Grasmere

Ullswater

Patterdale

Y

Haweswater

Shap

Orton

Kirkby Stephen

Y

Y

Keld

Complete walk → 190 miles

North Head, St Bees

Stonethwaite

Mount Grace Priory near Ingleby Cross

Robin Hood's Bay

A
COAST to COAST
WALK
Route indicated by a blue line

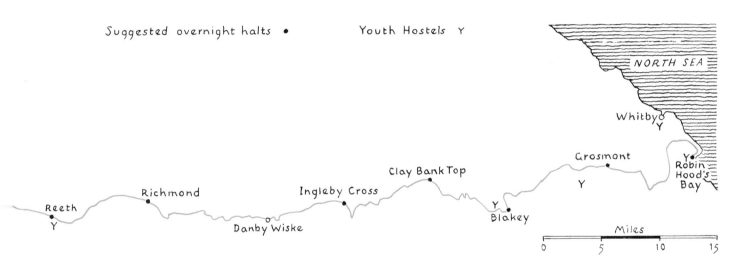

Suggested overnight halts •   Youth Hostels Y

NORTH SEA

Whitby Y

Grosmont
Y

Reeth
Y

Richmond

Clay Bank Top

Ingleby Cross

Danby Wiske

Y
Blakey

Y
Robin
Hood's
Bay

Miles

0   5   10   15

A corner of Reeth

Richmond Bridge

···· Acknowledgements ····

The author and publishers would like to thank *Westmorland Gazette* for permission to reproduce the line drawings which appear in the text and are taken from various books by A. Wainwright in which they hold the copyright.
The author and publishers would also like to thank Boris Weltman for redrawing the maps from original sketches.

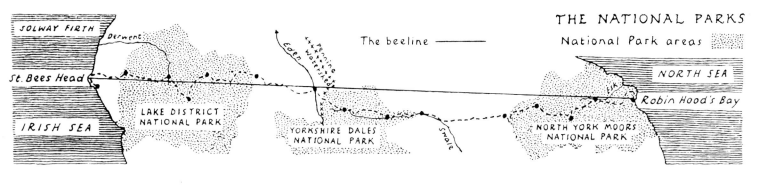

THE NATIONAL PARKS
National Park areas

SOLWAY FIRTH

Derwent

St. Bees Head

IRISH SEA

The beeline ————

LAKE DISTRICT NATIONAL PARK

Eden

Pennine Watershed

Swale

YORKSHIRE DALES NATIONAL PARK

NORTH SEA

Robin Hood's Bay

NORTH YORK MOORS NATIONAL PARK

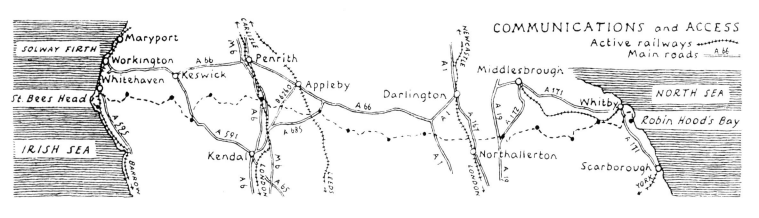

COMMUNICATIONS and ACCESS
Active railways ++++++++
Main roads ——— A 66

SOLWAY FIRTH

Maryport

Workington

Whitehaven

St. Bees Head

IRISH SEA

CARLISLE

M 6

A 66

Keswick

Penrith

A 6

B 6260

Appleby

A 591

A 6

A 685

Kendal

M 6

A 65

LONDON

A 6

LEEDS

Darlington

A 66

NEWCASTLE

A 1

A 167

A 1

LONDON

A 19

A 172

Middlesbrough

A 171

Whitby

NORTH SEA

Robin Hood's Bay

Northallerton

A 19

Scarborough

A 171

YORK

BARROW

A 595

ALTITUDES
(Vertical scale greatly exaggerated)
The highest point reached is Kidsty Pike, 2560' (between Patterdale and Shap)

feet		feet
2000		2000
1000		1000

South Head, St Bees

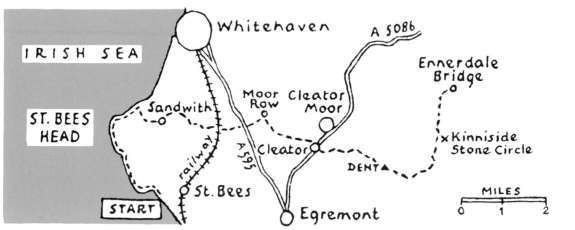

S AINT BEES, always abbreviated to St Bees, is a large village on the coast of Cumbria, four miles south of the port of Whitehaven and separated from it by a massive headland that thrusts into the Irish Sea and forms the most westerly point of northern England. Eight miles down the coast is the controversial nuclear power station of Sellafield, never long out of the news but too distant to affect seriously the life of the village. At St Bees, the coastline is indented to form a bay sheltered by the headland, the beach being a popular resort of visitors.

St Bees has proud religious and scholastic foundations, with a historical background dating from 650 AD when St Bega, an abbess, sailed from her native Ireland with a company of nuns in search of peace and solitude in England where they could dedicate their lives to the service of God. Their ship was wrecked on the rugged headland near the fishing village of Whitehaven, where they found shelter before travelling south along the valley of Pow Beck and arriving at a quiet place suitable for their purposes. Having lost their possessions in the wreck, they sought and obtained permission from the landowner to dwell there, and by industrious effort established a nunnery on the site of the present Priory Church at St Bees, this name being derived from Bega's and applied to the settlement that has since developed around the hallowed place she made her home.

Opposite *St Bees Bay from South Head*

The nunnery survived for two centuries before being destroyed by Danish raiders, after which the history of St Bees is obscure until 1120, when Henry I gave the land to a supporter who established a Priory on the same site as a cell of St Mary's, York, and endowed it bountifully. Then came a turbulent period during which the Priory suffered attacks from Scots raiders and subsequently met the fate of other monastic buildings and was dissolved by decree of Henry VIII.

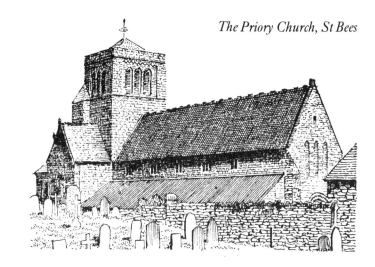

The Priory Church, St Bees

By this time, a community had developed around the Priory and the parishioners continued to worship in the ruins until 1611 when they started to undertake its restoration, adopting it as the Parish Church of St Mary and St Bega, the work going on until the nineteenth century. In 1817, the first Theological College in England was established in the chancel for the instruction of candidates for Holy Orders, but it was closed down in 1894.

The Church has interesting features and of special note is the Norman doorway, fortunately preserved throughout the many desecrations and deterioration of the fabric. It remains one of the finest examples of Norman architecture in the country. It is a joy to see, a thing of beauty, a work of art.

It is an inspiring prelude to the walk.

The Norman doorway, Priory Church

St Bees School

Below *Gateway to St Bees School*

St Bees also has strong scholastic traditions. In 1583, a Grammar School was founded here by the then Archbishop of Canterbury, a native of the district, under a charter from Elizabeth I. At first, it was intended for local boys only and continued to restrict admittance to such until 1879, when a new scheme was introduced to widen its educational opportunities and open its doors to others. Since then, the school has developed considerably, new buildings and boarding facilities being added. Today it enjoys national renown.

The school is entered through a beautiful memorial gate leading into a quadrangle, the whole complex being of handsome appearance and having extensive playing fields.

Sellafield from South Head

The walk to Robin Hood's Bay starts with an ascent and traverse of St Bees Head, a massive promontory three miles in length with cliffs that tower precipitously to a height of 300 feet above the pounding waters of the sea.

The beach at St Bees is half a mile from the village centre and is flanked by hotels and guest houses around an open expanse occupied by the parked cars and caravans of holiday-makers. A sea-wall, built to prevent erosion caused by high tides, leads to the abrupt end of the foreshore at a chaotic tumble of boulders fallen from impending cliffs, where a bathing pool hewn from the living rock is a popular amenity. Before leaving the beach, purists who are determined to walk every inch of the dry land between the two seas will perform the ritual of dipping their boots in the Irish Sea and hope to do the same in the North Sea in about a fortnight's time.

St Bees Head rises from the waves in two distinct sections, South Head and North Head, divided midway by the inlet of Fleswick Bay. The first objective is South Head and a much-frequented path ascends to it directly from the shore along the rising rim of precipitous cliffs, protected by a wire fence that marks the limit of pedestrian safety, the dangers of encroaching beyond being obvious. The cliffs are in a state of continuous erosion and the fence has repeatedly had to be moved back from the crumbling edge.

As height is gained, the views widen and far horizons appear. Along the coast to the south is the great whaleback of Black Combe beyond the tall towers and chimneys of Sellafield; to the east is the challenging skyline of the Lakeland fells, soon to be visited; and thirty miles distant to the west, the Isle of Man rises starkly from the shimmering sea.

Near the site of a dismantled coastguard hut, to the right of the path, is a curious fissure known as Pattering Holes, the subject of some improbable legends but more likely to have been merely used as badger setts.

When the gradient eases into the broad top of South Head – here named Tomlin Hill which unexpectedly, despite the exposed elevation, is patterned by fertile fields – North Head and its lighthouse come into sight in front. Walking is now an easy promenade on firm flowery turf, every step a delight and to the accompaniment of countless sea birds wheeling and darting across the cliff face, down which there are dramatic peeps to the thrashing waters far below. Next follows a long decline to the wonders of Fleswick Bay.

North Head and Fleswick Bay from South Head

Fleswick Bay

Fleswick Bay cuts across the route as a deep notch, circumvented by a sharp descent almost to sea level and re-ascent beyond, but the extra effort involved is fully rewarded by a short detour to the beach. Fleswick Bay is the most beautiful part of the headland, having a local fame for its attractive pebbles and being blessed with scenic charm: here in small compass are steep rocks with hanging gardens of flowers, caves, and intimate views of majestic cliffs. This is a compulsive place for the first halt of the day, and justified although less than two miles have so far been covered.

After climbing out of Fleswick Bay, the walk continues pleasantly as before alongside the warning fence. There is acute awareness of the sheer cliffs plunging down on the left, no longer the pure red sandstone of South Head but now displaying conglomerates of slate and coal and strata of white in the sandstone; littering the base are glacial erratics.

The ground rises gently to the lighthouse, standing just over 300 ft above the sea it commands and having a sturdy tower of 55 ft. The present building was erected in 1866 to replace other structures, the first being built in 1717. The interior may be inspected when convenient to the keeper. Nearby is a coastguard station.

The path continues around the butt end of the North Head, turning east to reveal the wide sweep of Saltom Bay and a first sighting of Whitehaven and its suburb Kells across the water. On the nearer skyline are the buildings and chimneys of a large chemical works. In the haze of distance, superimposed over the Solway Firth, are Criffell and the hills of Galloway.

The lighthouse, St Bees Head

Opposite *The cliffs of South Head*

Below *Saltom Bay*

Sandwith

When a large disused quarry is reached, the sea and the screaming gulls are left behind and lanes lead inland to the quiet village of Sandwith straggling a country road, with welcome trees and an air of rural tranquillity dispelled by the sight of the vast complex of chimneys and towers and sheds of the giant chemical works seen from Saltom Bay and dominating the landscape for miles around.

The environment has suffered by this enterprise, yet its development and rapid expansion has been a remarkable and romantic success story, bringing prosperity to a district that fell into severe depression between the wars with the decline in production of coal and iron on which the economy had been based. It was due to the initiative and foresight of mid-European industrialists, refugees from Hitler's régime, that this modern enterprise was introduced around 1940. A local mineral, anhydrite, long thought to be of little commercial value, forms the basis of its products of sulphuric acid and cement; also produced here are detergent chemicals and phosphates. The anhydrite mines penetrate far under St Bees Head.

These works have added nothing to the amenity and scenic values of the landscape and inevitably have further desecrated an area already badly scarred by the spoil heaps of abandoned iron-ore mines and smelting foundries and derelict railways. But West Cumbrians have compensation for a man-despoiled environment: in the background to their lives are the beautiful and undefiled fells of Lakeland.

At Sandwith there is a possibility of obtaining refreshments but eager feet, impelled by the beckoning hill of Dent ahead, the forerunner of Lakeland's fells, will lose no time indulging the inner man and press on towards this objective. First, however, the shallow valley of Pow Beck must be crossed, the next two miles being an intricate pattern of farm lanes and pastures intersected in turn by (a) the road linking St Bees and Whitehaven, carrying a bus service of which advantage can be taken by those whose gaze is not fixed exclusively on Dent to visit the large town and port of Whitehaven and see, in particular, its splendid harbour; (b) the main railway line (Lancaster—Whitehaven), reached at a pedestrian level crossing; and (c) the initial meanderings of Pow Beck.

The surroundings here are green and quite pleasant and a small lake, Stanley Pond, has resident swans, but there is a feeling in the air of urban influences and that the environs are merely the outskirts of Whitehaven, evidence of this being provided by the sprawling suburb of Hensingham only a few fields distant. Fields and cart tracks then lead up to a main road (Whitehaven—Egremont), also with a bus service. Looking back from this higher elevation, there is a last glimpse of St Bees, only two miles away although seven circuitous miles have been walked since leaving it.

Next on the itinerary is Moor Row, an industrial village reached along a side road. One feels sorry for Moor Row. In its heyday, it was a busy railway junction operating a network of lines, some for passengers, some servicing the iron ore and coal mines that pockmarked the area. There was a large railway station, engine shed and sidings, all now derelict; the mines have closed, and only the terraces of houses and built-up streets retain a fading atmosphere of Victorian industry and a few reminders of past glories.

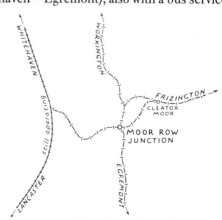

The derelict railways of Moor Row

A short mile beyond Moor Row is the next port of call, the old village of Cleator ('the outlying pasture among the rocks'), but it is no place to linger: this little community, too, has seen better days, expanding with the boom in iron-ore mining last century but in so doing sacrificing charm and character. Some architectural pretensions are evident in its places of worship and a few older houses, but are completely absent in the long terraces of small cottages built to a common pattern to provide for the rapid influx of miners. Brave attempts have been made to improve these dwellings but it needs more than tins of paint to make them visually attractive. The mines have closed; the homes of their workers remain amongst the scars as cheerless monuments to a brief prosperity that withered and died. Cleator, sadly, is typical of many West Cumbrian mining settlements similarly afflicted.

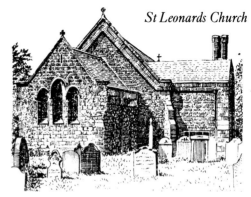

St Leonards Church

The parish church of Cleator, a neat building of red sandstone, is dedicated to St Leonard and although of modern appearance has twelfth-century masonry in its fabric from an earlier church on the site, and remains of even more ancient walls found here suggest a pre-Norman structure.

The good folk of Cleator are more concerned with earning a living than in catering for visitors, but the main road through the village goes south to Egremont (two miles; bus service), which has hotels and shops to meet all needs – and a ruined castle.

Cleator, however, has one feature that inspires sudden enthusiasm, for here is the River Ehen, coming from Ennerdale Water and heralding the start of Lakeland and the boundary of the National Park – and the traverse of the most beautiful part of the journey through the heart of its lovely mountains.

And dear little Dent, the first hill, is waiting nearby to introduce the wonderful territory that lies ahead.

Cleator, if nothing else, is a springboard to beauty.

The River Ehen at Cleator

Cleator is left at Blackhow Bridge over the Ehen. Here a lane rises to a farm and then a cart-track from which a long easy climb up the fellside, accompanied by a fence and later a broken wall, leads in mounting excitement to the cairn on the summit of Dent and the sudden revelation of a glorious prospect beyond.

View from Dent

Dent, once a deer park, is an excellent viewpoint with a panorama far more extensive than its modest elevation of 1131 ft would suggest. The whole of the coastal plain of Cumbria from Black Combe to the Solway is seen as on a map, without interruption, with a scattering of towns and villages, the scene being pleasant and the scars of industry erased by distance. The Isle of Man is fully in view, looking surprisingly near, and if visibility is really good it will be possible to settle an old argument as to whether the Irish mountains can be seen as the hills of Galloway certainly can. But attention will most be riveted on the great sweep of the Lakeland fells to the east, the prospect ranging clockwise from the Loweswater Fells overtopped by Skiddaw and Grasmoor to the High Stile and Pillar groups enclosing Ennerdale, and then, best of all, the fine silhouette of Scafell Pike. The only lake in view but not seen to full extent is Ennerdale Water. . . . How good it feels to be in Lakeland again!

A walker who has been exiled from the hills for some time and has missed the freedom and fresh air of the open spaces will depart from Dent reluctantly, for this miniature height has, in smaller measure, the charm and character of its grander neighbours and impels the same urge to linger awhile and let urban depression drain away. Dent is a small hill yet of great stature.

Raven Crag

The route continues down the east ridge of Dent into the quiet valley of Uldale, attractive despite its forests of conifers, and descends steeply alongside Raven Crag to the delectable hollow of Nannycatch Gate.

There are many hidden corners of Lakeland, off the beaten tracks of tourists and rarely visited, that are gems of scenic charm in settings of undisturbed peace yet never get a mention in guidebooks. Amongst these, in fact topping the list, is Nannycatch Gate, a delightful and unexpected sylvan glade where three crystal becks join forces beneath the ramparts of Raven Crag in a narrow defile threaded by an enchanting path, a favourite with pony trekkers and with discerning walkers who love solitude and are well content to hear only the murmur of streams and the singing of birds. Nannycatch is a secret retreat.

Three views of Nannycatch

The valley path is followed alongside the descending Nannycatch Beck in a deep ravine below the long escarpment of Flat Fell. On easy ground at the head of the defile, where wide landscapes are again in view, the moorland motor road coming over Cold Fell from Calder Bridge is joined and crossed for an inspection of the Kinniside Stone Circle directly opposite.

Kinniside Stone Circle

This circle has been the subject of conjecture and doubts and its authenticity has been questioned. For a long time, the story was accepted that the original stones had been removed by local farmers to use as walling material but that early this century they had been retrieved and replaced in their sockets by outraged historians. This story is now regarded as a fib, the true facts being, so it is claimed, that the stones were arranged on this site merely as an example of a prehistoric stone circle by a local archaeologist. Significantly there is no mention of it on Ordnance Survey maps.

A long mile down the road is the cluster of buildings forming the small village of Ennerdale Bridge, acquaintance with the River Ehen being here resumed. Most walkers will now feel they have done enough for the first day and accept one of the beds and breakfasts on offer. Youth hostellers will probably prefer to go on to the hostels in Ennerdale.

Tomorrow, Lakeland proper!

Ennerdale
Bridge
Ennerdale
Water
RED PIKE
o Buttermere
Buttermere
Rosthwaite
YH o
Seatoller
HIGH
STYLE
HIGH CRAG
Honister
YH
HAYSTACKS
High Gillerthwaite
YH   River Liza
PILLAR
Ennerdale
Black
Sail YH
GREAT GABLE

MILES
0   1   2

THE NEXT stage of the walk leads along the shore of Ennerdale Water and enters Ennerdale Forest, a vast conifer plantation that has sprouted over the past fifty years and extends for several miles to the head of the valley where the route climbs over open fell country to reach Honister and the most beautiful of all valleys, Borrowdale. Two of Lakeland's giants, Pillar and Great Gable, dominate this section, the mountain scenery being dramatic and exciting. Paths are distinct throughout and no problems of route-finding should arise even in mist or rain.

A fine-weather alternative, strongly recommended for energetic walkers, varies part of the route by a traverse of the High Stile range, one of the finest high-level ridges in the district with views of superlative beauty.

Either way there is no chance of buying refreshments and the rucksack should carry enough goodies for a long day.

Ennerdale Bridge is left by the Croasdale road, from which a quiet lane branches off to cross a bridge over the River Ehen near a pumping station and ancillary waterworks, and then quite suddenly and with an overpowering impact on the senses, Ennerdale Water is revealed in all its glory as an expansive sheet of water encompassed by colourful fellsides, with shadowy mountains beyond its furthest reaches.

This is a wonderful moment, a vista of grandeur. This is Lakeland!

The River Ehen near the pumping station

Ennerdale Water

Ennerdale Water is the most westerly of the lakes and not usually included in tourist itineraries. However, it is frequented by day visitors from the coastal towns nearby and has popular camping sites. It is a fisherman's lake noted for its brown trout and char.

The water authorities of the region have for years cast covetous eyes on Ennerdale Water. Water is at present extracted, but unobtrusively. More ambitious proposals for increasing the capacity of the lake by raising the water level and constructing a longer and higher weir and embankments were recently introduced but strongly opposed by conservationist bodies and rejected after a lengthy Public Inquiry. Rightly so. The proposals would have permanently damaged the landscape, drowning the vegetation along the shores and submerging waterside paths. Ennerdale has already suffered enough from commercial exploitation. Haweswater, on the eastern fringe of the district, is a shameful example of the effect of converting a natural lake into a reservoir and we want no more. Lakeland is far too precious to be robbed of the unique qualities that make it so.

Either side of the lake may be followed to its head, the north side having crowds and campers and car parks, the south side solitude. It is an easy decision to make. The south side, of course.

Angler's Crag   *Crag Fell Pinnacles*

The shore path starts at once from the outflow and is soon confronted by the promontory of Angler's Crag barring direct progress. The path circumvents this obstacle by climbing alongside to its grassy top and descending on the far side to regain the shore. The top of the crag is a splendid viewpoint, the head of the lake, the valley beyond and the massive Pillar range now being fully in view. Nearer, across the lake, is seen the Anglers' Hotel, not standing where it formerly stood, so close to the water's edge that residents could fish from its windows, but since rebuilt at a higher elevation behind in anticipation of the flood that never came.

Also glimpsed from this eminence, much higher on the fellside, are the Crag Fell Pinnacles, a curious formation unique in the district, where a curtain of rock has fractured and splintered into vertical pillars, the highest being 80 ft tall and seemingly unassailable. Still further up the fellside, and rimming the skyline, is the long escarpment of Revelin Crag.

This detour over the top of Angler's Crag can be avoided by threading a tortuous passage through the fallen rocks at the base of the crag. Here is a small headland named on old maps as Robin Hood's Chair, a name that has gone out of use but is worthy of note by walkers bound for his Bay on the East Coast.

Beyond, the path is rejoined and continues uneventfully to the head of the lake.

Robin Hood's Chair

Pillar from Ennerdale Water

The mountains ahead and on both flanks of the valley are now very impressive, forming a great amphitheatre, Pillar being the dominant height. A deep, wooded ravine coming down on the right discloses the long skyline of the Scoat Fell ridge, and high on the left are the forerunners of the High Stile range.

At the extremity of the lake level pastures are crossed to a footbridge over the inflow, the River Liza, and then the forest road up the valley is joined.

All lovers of trees will feel like weeping at the prospect immediately ahead. Here is afforestation gone mad, totally insensitive to amenity values and with no regard to the natural growth and development of trees. Here they are grown as poles, closely packed and deprived of light – a million miserable cripples with withered arms and no joy in living. Here is battery forestry with all the attendant evils of mass production. Every one of these trees wanted to be a proud specimen but is condemned to a slow death from infancy. The areas of planting have been drawn with a ruler on the map, the forest boundaries being in straight lines, confining the wretched inmates in regimented ranks without freedom even to stretch their limbs. Ennerdale Forest is a concentration camp.

There were objections when the plan to afforest Ennerdale was decided upon about fifty years ago, but to no avail. Yet how right the conservationists have been proved! The charm of the valley has been destroyed beyond redemption. A blight has descended on it.

There can be few of us left who knew Ennerdale as it used to be, and as it was meant to be. I remember walking along the valley one February day in the early 1930s. The track then was rudimentary, with potholes holding little pools after recent rain and occupied by mating frogs. Except for the windbreaks sheltering the two farms of Gillerthwaite, the valley was bare and desolate yet had a sombre beauty: the tawny grasses, the green mosses, the russet-gold of dead bracken and the grey rocks and boulders added colour even under a leaden sky. All this was to change. For the worse.

Ennerdale Forest

The forest road leading up the valley is now followed and it will be noticed that the lower slopes of the adjoining fells have also been given unbecoming skirts of dark conifers, not a pretty sight.

The Youth Hostel at High Gillerthwaite is soon reached, and just beyond is a welcome break in the plantations on the left up which climbs a sketchy path bound for Red Pike 2000 ft above. This is the point where the recommended fine-weather alternative turns off, and the narrative will return to it after describing the main route as far as the reunion of the two routes at the site of Drum House above Honister.

Road in Ennerdale Forest

The River Liza in Ennerdale Forest

The main route, the safer in adverse weather conditions, continues forward along the forest road, tedious mile after tedious mile of very easy walking in an avenue of spruces that, with the advantage of daylight provided by the swathe of the road, have been allowed to develop normally unlike their poor brethren behind. Only occasionally is there a clear glimpse of the rocky ramparts high on both sides, but in a few places it is possible to cross to the river running alongside and to break the dead silence of the forest, which has no birds and therefore no bird-song, by listening to the happy and harmonious music of the racing waters: the Liza at least has refused to kow-tow to forestry operations and maintained its age-long independence throughout the journey from its birthplace on Great Gable.

After what seems an eternity in the close company of spruces, there is a welcome return to full daylight and open views at the forest boundary fence, the roadway going on to Black Sail Hut, the loneliest of all Youth Hostels in Lakeland, built originally as a shepherd's bothy and little changed in appearance.

Black Sail Hut

For mountain adventurers with a Y.H.A. card, there is no better centre than this. The situation is dramatic, in a surround of challenging yet beckoning peaks. Pillar, Great Gable, High Crag and Haystacks all look down on the humble building and offer sporting tracks to their summits, and two much-travelled paths leave its doors, one going over Scarth Gap to Buttermere and the other crossing Black Sail Pass to Wasdale Head. It is good to be young in heart and temporarily billeted at Black Sail Hut.

The route follows neither of the usual escapes from the valley but continues forward into the head of the valley, passing an area rippled by drumlins, small rounded hummocks left behind by the glacier that once filled the valley. Directly ahead, Great Gable is a magnificent sight.

Half a mile beyond the hut, Loft Beck comes down on the left to join the Liza. The path climbs alongside, initially very steep and calling for halts amply justified by the commanding presence of Great Gable, becoming more impressive as height is gained, and by the retrospect of Ennerdale, its forest boundaries now seen clearly delineated with the river appearing as a silver thread through the dark shroud of conifers, and Pillar towering majestically above.

Great Gable   Opposite *Ennerdale from Loft Beck*

The uphill progress alongside Loft Beck gradually eases and the path trends to the right across good ground, with a delectable view of the Buttermere valley opening up on the left, and joins a well-blazed track at a large cairn. This is Moses' Trod, today a popular way to Great Gable from Honister but originating as a commercial route regularly used by a Honister quarryman, Moses Rigg, to convey his pony-loads of slate over the fells to Wasdale and Ravenglass. Moses, however, was an entrepreneur who after his day's work at the quarry stayed behind and distilled his own brand of whisky from the bog water on Fleetwith and smuggled his potent produce in his loads of slate. He was a man of initiative and resource, and his spare-time industry, although illegal, has earned for his name 150 years of immortality as modern walkers tread in his steps along the path still known as Moses' Trod.

The Buttermere Valley, from Moses' Trod

From the junction of paths it is a simple downhill stroll, made highly enjoyable by a glorious vista of Buttermere and Crummock Water, to the site of the old Drum House of Honister Quarry, where another path joins from the west. If companions have preferred the alternative route from Gillerthwaite, this is the place to wait for them. They will appear along the path from the west within the next two hours enthusing about their experiences on the High Stile range.

The narrative here returns to Gillerthwaite to describe, mainly by photographs, the superior delights of the alternative route.

From the forest road near Gillerthwaite, the break in the plantations is ascended to the open fellside above the tree-line, the path being unremittingly steep with no features of interest in the immediate vicinity but affording aerial views of Ennerdale and a greater appreciation of the towering bulk of Pillar on the other side, its long summit escarpment and the famous Pillar Rock now being seen in better perspective.

Pillar, seen from the path to Red Pike

The path scores a bullseye by arriving precisely at the top cairn of Red Pike, and the tedium of the long climb is immediately forgotten as a view of exquisite beauty suddenly unfolds, the ground collapsing dramatically to reveal the Buttermere valley far below and range after range of lofty mountains beyond: a superb prospect.

The ridge to be followed is now seen curving around the cliffs of Bleaberry Comb and rising to the next summit, High Stile, with Pillar still towering above the great gulf of Ennerdale and between them a glimpse of the Scafell group, the highest ground in England.

This is the greatest moment of the walk thus far and a prelude to one of the most attractive high-level traverses in the district. Two hours of thrilling and exciting situations are ahead with the camera working overtime.

The summit of High Stile

Easy walking from Red Pike gives way to rough scrambling up a bouldery slope, with impressive peeps down the steep declivities of Chapel Crags to Bleaberry Tarn inurned far below, and then the summit rocks and cairn of High Stile are reached, disclosing a magnificent panoramic view guaranteed to stop all walkers in their tracks.

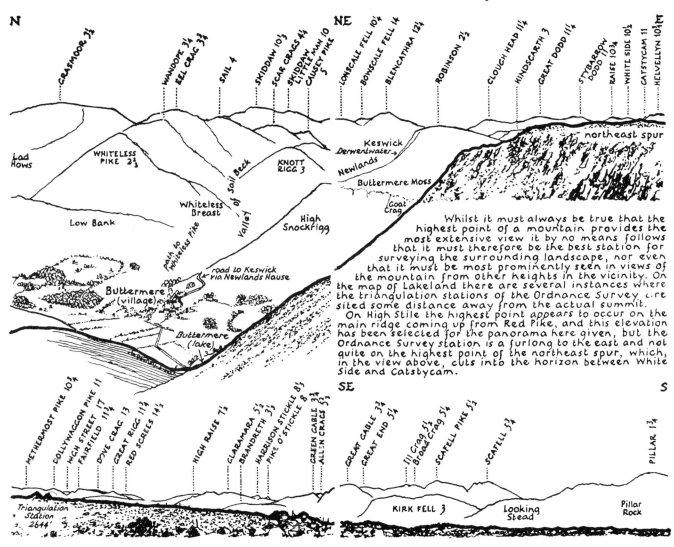

N

NE

GRASMOOR 2½
WANDOPE 3¼
EEL CRAG 3½
SAIL 4
SKIDDAW 10⅓
SCAR CRAGS 4¼
SKIDDAW LITTLE MAN 10
CAUSEY PIKE 5
LONSCALE FELL 10¼
BONSCALE FELL 14
BLENCATHRA 12¼
ROBINSON 2½
CLOUGH HEAD 11¼
HINDSCARTH 3
GREAT DODD 11¼
STYBARROW DODD
RAISE 10¾
WHITE SIDE 10½
CATSTYCAM 11
HELVELLYN 10½

Lad Hows
WHITELESS PIKE 2⅓
KNOTT RIGG 3
Keswick
Derwentwater
Newlands
Buttermere Moss
Goat Crag
northeast spur

Whiteless Breast
Low Bank
Valley of Sail Beck
High Snockrigg
path to Whiteless Pike
road to Keswick via Newlands Hause
Buttermere (village)
Buttermere (lake)

Whilst it must always be true that the highest point of a mountain provides the most extensive view it by no means follows that it must therefore be the best station for surveying the surrounding landscape, nor even that it must be most prominently seen in views of the mountain from other heights in the vicinity. On the map of Lakeland there are several instances where the triangulation stations of the Ordnance Survey are sited some distance away from the actual summit.

On High Stile the highest point appears to occur on the main ridge coming up from Red Pike, and this elevation has been selected for the panorama here given, but the Ordnance Survey station is a furlong to the east and not quite on the highest point of the northeast spur, which, in the view above, cuts into the horizon between White Side and Catstycam.

SE

S

NETHERMOST PIKE 10¾
COLLYWAGGON PIKE 11
HIGH STREET 17
FAIRFIELD 11¾
DOVE CRAG 13
GREAT RIGG 11¾
RED SCREES 14¼
HIGH RAISE 7½
GLARAMARA 5½
BRANDRETH 3⅓
HARRISON STICKLE 8⅓
PIKE O'STICKLE 8
GREEN GABLE 3¾
ALLEN CRAGS 5½
GREAT GABLE 3¾
GREAT END 5¼
ILL CRAG 5½
BROAD CRAG 5¼
SCAFELL PIKE 5½
SCAFELL 5¾
PILLAR 1¾

Triangulation Station 2644'
KIRK FELL 3
Looking Stead
Pillar Rock

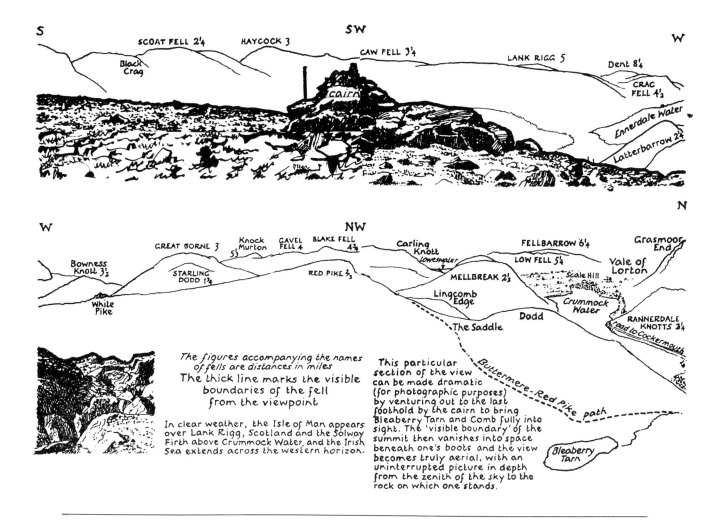

S
SCOAT FELL 2¼   HAYCOCK 3   SW   CAW FELL 3¼   LANK RIGG 5   W
Black Crag   Dent 8¼
CRAG FELL 4½
cairn
Ennerdale Water
Latterbarrow 2¼

W   NW   N
Knock   GAVEL   BLAKE FELL   Carling   FELLBARROW 6¼   Grasmoor End
GREAT BORNE 3   Murton   FELL 4   4½   Knott   LOW FELL 5¼   Vale of Lorton
53   Lowesmater   Scale Hill
Bowness Knott 3½   STARLING DODD 1¾   RED PIKE ⅔   MELLBREAK 2½   Crummock Water
White Pike   Lingcomb Edge   Dodd   RANNERDALE KNOTTS 2¼
The Saddle   road to Cockermouth

The figures accompanying the names of fells are distances in miles
The thick line marks the visible boundaries of the fell from the viewpoint

In clear weather, the Isle of Man appears over Lank Rigg, Scotland and the Solway Firth above Crummock Water, and the Irish Sea extends across the western horizon.

This particular section of the view can be made dramatic (for photographic purposes) by venturing out to the last foothold by the cairn to bring Bleaberry Tarn and Comb fully into sight. The 'visible boundary' of the summit then vanishes into space beneath one's boots and the view becomes truly aerial, with an uninterrupted picture in depth from the zenith of the sky to the rock on which one stands.

Buttermere-Red Pike path
Bleaberry Tarn

High Stile, at 2644 ft, is the most elevated place on the ridge and has the greatest stature, its extensive slopes falling sharply into Buttermere, and a lengthy halt to gaze upon the array of peaks all around is inevitable. There is so much to see.

Resuming the walk, the cliffs of Burtness Comb are skirted to the next summit, High Crag, also a fine viewpoint. Then, maintaining the same direction, the loose screes of Gamlin End are descended with care and the minor height of Seat rounded to reach and cross the pedestrian highway of Scarth Gap and mount the rough facing slope to the abrupt summit of Haystacks and fresh delights.

Words are woefully inadequate to describe the bewitching loveliness of the section of the route from High Stile to Haystacks, and here I hand over to Derry for a few pages to let him try to convey with his camera a visual impression of this part of the journey.

Opposite *Crummock Water and Bleaberry Tarn from High Street*

Fleetwith Pike from High Stile
Pillar from High Stile

Burtness Comb
The head of Ennerdale from High Crag

Opposite *Haystacks from High Crag*

The Drum House, in its prime, operated the cable of a tramway used for conveying slate from the nearby Honister quarries down to the cutting sheds below. This tramway, today a river of loose stones, is now adapted by walkers and provides an uncomfortable descent to the motor road on the summit of Honister Pass, where there is a Youth Hostel and a complex of quarry sheds in which the slate is cut. From here, the near-vertical precipice of Honister Crag is seen in striking profile, its steep face an amazing network of quarry roads and paths. The slate which is produced from a honeycomb of holes in the crag is a beautiful colour, durable, and of great renown.

Now for Borrowdale. The motor road is followed east until a former highway, now grass-grown and abandoned, branches off on the left. This was the Toll Road and it provides a pleasant traffic-free descent to the valley at Seatoller (meals and refreshments) where there is a welcome reunion with handsome trees growing as Nature intended them to grow. Here are trees to be admired, not pitied as in Ennerdale.

Honister Crag

Seatoller

Borrowdale is the very heart of the Lake District and here the romantic loveliness of the region is fully displayed. It is the most beautiful of the valleys, fair to look upon throughout its length from the colourful mountains at its head to the charming lake of Derwentwater in its lower reaches. Everywhere is a mystic delight that dims the eyes with tears of joy and uplifts the spirit in exultation. Its great appeal is that it is unorthodox, following no pattern but forming a haphazard landscape of craggy outcrops, verdant woodlands and emerald pastures watered by a crystal river, of hanging gardens of rowan and birch above a floor of mature oaks, with a scattering of white cottages and farmhouses that in no way intrudes but fits perfectly into a picture of rural tranquillity. Nature has been bountiful in Borrowdale: this is its showplace, a heaven on earth.

The manifold attractions of Borrowdale make it very popular and in summer crowds and cars throng the valley roads. I remember Borrowdale before its peace was disturbed by tourists. There were few cars then, and its visitors were conveyed in a little bus that shuttled between Keswick and Seatoller in the care of a driver of great character whose proud boast was that he never left anyone stranded at a bus stop or indeed anywhere along the road but crushed all his passengers in somehow, often in extreme discomfort, duly arriving in Keswick with his bus bursting at the seams and bodies hanging out of the open door. Those were happy days, jolly days. Sometimes I think they were better days. . .

But I suppose one should not complain about people from the towns wanting a glimpse of a natural paradise. They are, after all, only ants in the rich tapestry of Borrowdale.

The road from Seatoller goes down the valley, making brief acquaintance with the River Derwent and passing yet another Youth Hostel and soon reaches Rosthwaite, the 'capital' of Borrowdale, a small community with a long experience of catering for visitors. Here are many hotels and guest houses. A good place to rest weary limbs. And a rare chance to sleep in Arcadia.

Rosthwaite

ROSTHWAITE to GRASMERE : 9¼ miles

B 5289

Rosthwaite

Stonethwaite

EAGLE CRAG   ULLSCARF burn

Greenup Edge   ALF CRAG
                GIBSON KNOTT

HIGH RAISE   Far Easedale   HELM CRAG

Wythburn

MILES
0   1   2

Grasmere

A 591

TRAVEL ON foot amongst the fells should always be leisurely. Slow progress is enforced by the roughness or absence of paths, but a more compelling reason for frequent halts is the infinite variety of the scenery, the intimate delights, the landscapes and the views that are presented along the way. Beauty is too rare to be hurried past. And Lakeland, of all places, ought to be savoured slowly.

The next twenty miles lie across the central area of Lakeland and are described in two sections, each having a simple up-and-down progression that could be walked comfortably in half a day but deserve a lingering acquaintance. The first follows a distinct path over the pass of Greenup Edge to Grasmere, but for energetic walkers a rather more strenuous alternative midway is suggested.

Rosthwaite is left by the river bridge and a path followed into the secluded side-valley of Stonethwaite alongside a tributary of the River Derwent in surroundings with the true Lakeland flavour. I venture the opinion that this lovely side-valley and the hamlet of Stonethwaite (reached by crossing a bridge), backed by the abrupt tower of Eagle Crag, is most representative of the romantic charm of Lakeland.

The first bewitching mile, every step a joy, is an idyllic journey.

Left *Stonethwaite*
Opposite *Eagle Crag from the Stonethwaite Valley*

After passing the wide opening of Langstrath and a delightful meeting of sparkling waters, the environs become austere as the path climbs steadily, passing Eagle Crag and later rounding Lining Crag, to reach its highest point at the pass of Greenup Edge, a bare and shelterless crossing that opens up a wide view forward, welcome after the close confinement of the path during the ascent. Beyond, in thick weather, there is a danger of going astray by turning alongside descending streams on the left under the impression that they will point the way to Grasmere, but the streams actually drain a valley that emerges at Wythburn. In clear conditions, there should be no problem: the path contours around the head of this valley and ascends a slight rise to another pass formerly crossed by a wire fence of which only an iron stile still remains. This point is the head of Far Easedale, leading directly to Grasmere, and the place where a decision must be made.

Looking down from Gibson Knott into Far Easedale

There is now a choice of routes.

The main route, designed to defeat bad weather, keeps to the path descending into Far Easedale, a rough and pleasant way down in the company of a tumbling beck, becoming sophisticated when the track becomes a tarred road passing some handsome residences and leading into Grasmere village: this route is straightforward and foolproof and needs no further directions.

The alternative, strongly recommended in fine weather, follows the ridge on the north side of Far Easedale, is more interesting, has better views, demands only a little extra effort and is little longer in time and distance.

The summit rocks, Calf Crag

This alternative aims first for the top of Calf Crag, reached up an easy slope half left and then follows the ridge on an enchanting track to the next objective, Gibson Knott, before descending in heather to a grassy depression with Helm Crag, a shapely pyramid, beyond. The path goes steeply up to its exciting summit.

Helm Crag from Gibson Knott

The summit rocks of Helm Crag

Helm Crag is the best known, by sight, of all the Lakeland heights and instantly identified even by tourists who have never visited its rocky top and have no interest in fellwalking. Silhouetted against the sky when viewed from the main road leaving Grasmere for Keswick are the rocks known to all as the Lion and the Lamb, greeted with shouts of recognition by passengers in cars and coaches.

The rocky crest of the summit, only a hundred yards or so in length and a mere 1300 ft in height, is nevertheless the most distinguished of all Lakeland tops. Most prominent of its features is the sloping pinnacle, poised above a sheer drop, known as the Howitzer when seen from Dunmail Raise and as the Old Woman at the Organ from lower down the road. The rocks forming the Lion and the Lamb are at the Grasmere end of the summit ridge but less easily identified when alongside.

Helm Crag has another distinction. It is the only Lakeland summit on which I have never stood. The top inch of the pinnacle is the highest point on the fell and although I have been assured that this massive upthrust of naked rock can be scaled without much difficulty by anybody with a steady head, I have never ventured to climb up to its topmost inch. The situation is too airy for me. I do have a steady head but not as steady as all that.

The Howitzer, Helm Crag

The Lion and the Lamb rocks are passed as the summit is left, the path then descending along the ridge to its extremity, which is rounded to join a steep and slippery slope of loose stones that used to be a path, now scoured out of existence by overmuch foot-traffic, Helm Crag being a popular place of pilgrimage by sojourners at Grasmere: so bad is the erosion here that the Park wardens have made a new path to supplant the old.

At the bottom of the slope the Far Easedale road is met and Grasmere is only minutes away.

Almost everybody knows Grasmere or has heard of it. This is the Lakeland village most often visited, cars and coaches arriving in daily processions throughout the year. The attractions of

The Lion and the Lamb

Grasmere are many: apart from a lovely setting in a bowl of the fells, there is a lake with boating facilities, shops and studios, the most famous of all Lakeland sporting events, graves of great men in the churchyard, flower gardens, and above all Dove Cottage where Wordsworth lived.

Grasmere is no longer the haven of peace it used to be. Visitors are catered for on a grand scale: there are many hotels and boarding houses plus a Youth Hostel. The streets are thronged with sightseers. The village has become a place for those who are happiest in crowds; the loner will find a quick bed and breakfast and depart in a hurry without looking back.

Wordsworth's grave

Dove Cottage

Below *Grasmere Church*

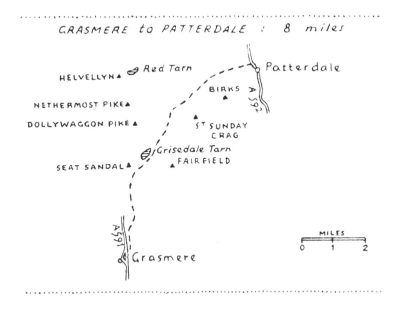

GRASMERE to PATTERDALE : 8 miles

HELVELLYN▲ ⌀ Red Tarn   ● Patterdale
                        BIRKS
NETHERMOST PIKE▲   ▲
DOLLYWAGGON PIKE▲   ST SUNDAY
                       CRAG
                ⌀ Grisedale Tarn
SEAT SANDAL▲   FAIRFIELD
                       ▲

                              MILES
                         0   1   2

A591 ⌀ Grasmere

THIS SECTION is a counterpart to the last: a straightforward walk on a well-defined path rising to a high pass and then descending a long valley.

To add a spice of mountain adventure, two alternative finishes are described, one (over Helvellyn) requiring extra effort and increasing the distance by two miles, the other (over St Sunday Crag) being less arduous and only a little longer. Neither of these alternatives should be considered in adverse weather conditions.

A mile out of Grasmere on the A.591, a signpost points the way to a path that rises gently until confronted by the formidable slope of Great Tongue, avoided by rounding it on either side. The usual route is to the left along a path devised for ponies hired by Victorian ladies and gentlemen to take them to the top of Helvellyn: this climbs tediously on grass before contouring along the flank of Seat Sandal to reach the pass of Grisedale Hause after a final rocky rise. The right-hand route, easier initially, ends with a steep and loose climb, passing waterfalls, to join the other just below the Hause.

The views thus far have been restricted to the retrospect but at the Hause a fresh landscape is suddenly disclosed, Dollywaggon Pike appearing ahead with the Helvellyn path seen zigzagging up its arid breast and, below and within a stone's throw, the waters of Grisedale Tarn.

From the Hause a stony track descends to skirt the shore of the tarn and arrive at the outlet, a favourite halt. On the bouldery slope beyond is the rock known as Brothers Parting, where Wordsworth said a last farewell to his brother John, an event commemorated by verses on a tablet affixed.

The outlet of the tarn is the place for contemplating the weather, the time of day and the state of the blisters. This is a crossroads where a choice has to be made between three alternative routes.

The first and obvious one continues along the path, descending gradually to Ruthwaite Lodge, formerly a shooting hut, and then steeply to the floor of Grisedale, deep-set between the Helvellyn range and St Sunday Crag in impressive surroundings, the last few miles on a cart-track that becomes a tarred road going down between woodlands to Patterdale. This is the main route and the only one to consider in rain or mist.

Dollywaggon Pike from Grisedale

Nethermost Pike from Grisedale

Opposite *Grisedale Tarn*

Helvellyn from Nethermost Pike   Opposite *Striding Edge*

The Helvellyn alternative is for walkers who consider themselves to be supremely fit and are encouraged by weather conditions that invite a detour to one of the highest and most frequented of Lakeland summits.

The first stage of the ascent is not at all promising, the climb to Dollywaggon Pike being a weary treadmill lacking interest, but spirits rise when the gradient eases to give simple walking. The path bypasses the domed summit of the Pike which, however, is worth a visit and follows the edge of an escarpment to the level plateau of Nethermost Pike, its highest point also bypassed, and then the 3000-ft contour is crossed on a steady rise to the top of Helvellyn, 3118 ft high.

Throughout the walk, far-reaching views over a tumult of peaks in the west will have been enjoyed and from the ultimate height of Helvellyn are even more extensive, the all-round panorama being crowded with distant detail including a first sighting of Ullswater.

The next objective is the notorious Striding Edge, reached by a steep and stony slide on loose scree from Gough's Memorial, which commemorates a man killed by a fall from the Edge in 1803, his dead body being guarded by his faithful dog for three months before it was found: an example of canine fidelity that inspired poems by Wordsworth and Scott.

Striding Edge looks fearful, but its dangers are more apparent than real. There is an awkward scramble to set foot on it, but thereafter a thin track a few feet below the actual crest gives a safe passage to the rock tower at the extremity of the Edge and the easy ground beyond: another memorial passed midway is a reminder to exercise care, especially in a gusty wind or when the rocks are sheathed in ice.

With Striding Edge safely negotiated, the remainder of the descent to Patterdale will seem by comparison a highway for toddlers. A path continues along the declining ridge, now free from perils, before slanting down the flank of Birkhouse Moor as another Victorian pony track with glorious aerial views of the full length of Grisedale beneath the towering cliffs of St Sunday Crag. At the foot of the slope, Grisedale Beck is crossed by a bridge and the tarred road joined for the last pleasant mile into Patterdale village.

Grisedale

The cliffs of Fairfield

The other alternative from Grisedale Tarn has as its main feature the complete traverse of St Sunday Crag, this requiring less effort than a visit to Helvellyn with no problems of route-finding and having as its reward, apart from the invigorating exercise of walking on rough ground, a classic view of Ullswater. But in this case too, fine clear weather is essential for enjoyment.

Looking from the outlet of the tarn, St Sunday Crag is seen soaring above Grisedale on the right, its upper slopes springing from a depression in the skyline, Deepdale Hause, linking the mountain with the neighbouring and nearer height of Fairfield. A slanting beeline is made to the Hause. There was no path to it in my younger days but on a recent visit I noticed that a sketchy track had formed and this, if found, eases the ascent.

On arrival at the Hause, a splendid view of the cliffs of Fairfield, terminating in the steep buttress of Greenhow End, is revealed, with the upper reaches of the valley of Deepdale winding away below.

A steady climb up a broad ridge reaches the tilted plateau forming the top of St Sunday Crag, the rather featureless ascent being compensated by a striking view across the great gulf of Grisedale, now far below, of the massive build-up of the Helvellyn range.

Helvellyn from St Sunday Crag   Opposite *Ullswater*

The summit, at 2756 ft, is a place of mosses and lichens and grey rocks with two cairns, and unexciting. The long fringe of crags overlooking Grisedale remains unseen and the main interest is centred on the glorious view of Ullswater, becoming ever more beautiful as the summit is crossed and the ridge descends to an outcropping of striated rocks. This is a better prospect than anything Helvellyn can provide and one of my special favourite Lakeland views. I could sit and look at it for hours.

Opposite *View from Boardale Hause*

Above *Kirkstone Pass*

The path continues to rise steadily, passing Boardale Hause and its ruined chapel and, further, the head of the ravine of Dubhow Beck, where there is a view down to Brothers Water. The rocky top of Angletarn Pikes is next rounded suddenly to reveal Angle Tarn ahead in a green hollow. The path descends to skirt the eastern shore of this attractive sheet of water and rises again beyond.

Angle Tarn

The view ahead from Satura Crag

Opposite, top: *Riggindale from the Straits*

The path halts its upward progress on Satura Crag and here can be seen the wide sweep of fells still to be crossed, a broad expanse of undulating upland, bare and inhospitable, rising to well-defined summits and cut by deep valleys, with a lofty skyline closing the view. This is confusing territory and it is fortunate that the path remains distinct underfoot aiming for The Knott and rounding it steeply to arrive at a depression in the skyline known as the Straits of Riggindale.

Here is historic ground, the Roman road linking Ambleside and Brougham being met as it comes down from High Street on its 25-mile journey north. This road, now used as a walkers' path, was the highest engineered by the Romans in this country, maintaining an elevation of more than 2000 ft for several continuous miles, and is a permanent memorial to the skill of their surveyors and the endurance of the legions who marched along it in all weathers.

Also hereabouts may be seen some of the creatures that inhabit the eastern fells. Red deer from their sanctuary in nearby Martindale have freedom to roam and herds may often be seen grazing on the higher slopes. Half-wild fell ponies, docile yet hardy animals that can survive the cruellest winter, are a common sight. Rough fell sheep are everywhere, and there are occasional glimpses of a lone fox. But the greatest thrill is the soaring flight of one of Lakeland's golden eagles, recently returned to this part of the district after an absence of 150 years.

The Straits of Riggindale are precisely at the head of the valley of that name down which there is a vista of Mardale and Haweswater, distant yet but soon to be visited.

The route now follows in the steps of the Romans up the ridge to the left until abreast of the peaked top of Kidsty Pike, to which a level track branches off, affording an uninterrupted view across the depths of Riggindale to the great mass of High Street.

It was on the uppermost rocks of Kidsty Pike that, a few years ago, I saw an eagle alight after an effortless crossing from the crags of High Street half a mile away, the flight being accomplished in ten seconds by two lazy flaps of the wings. It was a sight that made my day.

High Street, from Kidsty Pike

Kidsty Pike is a milestone on the journey. It is the highest point reached by the main route, and the last place to offer a final look at the fells of Lakeland, now arrayed on the western horizon, among which the past few days have been spent. It is a sad farewell.

But they have not gone forever. They will await further visits in the future and, unlike so much else, they will not change. Say 'so long', not goodbye.

The walk continues from Kidsty Pike down a declining ridge that erupts in an outcropping of rocks on Kidsty Howes, and here can be seen half a mile distant the walled ruins of the ancient British fort on Birks Crag, outlined against Haweswater. But it is the prospect ahead of Mardale Head in a mountain surround that most catches the eye.

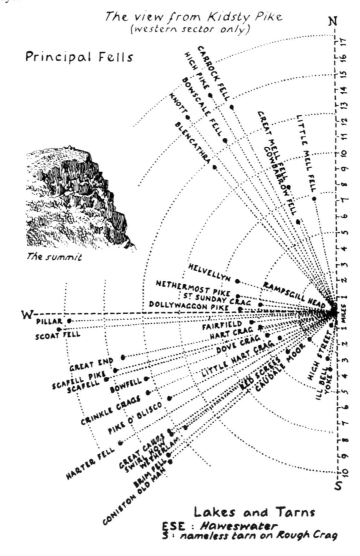

The view from Kidsty Pike
(western sector only)

Principal Fells

The summit

Lakes and Tarns
ESE : Haweswater
S : nameless tarn on Rough Crag

It is strange how some experiences remain vivid in the memory, and others, although contemporary, quickly fade. I well remember being in Mardale Head one lovely summer day in the late 1930s but have now no recollection of my route of approach to it, presumably over Gatescarth Pass or Nan Bield, nor where my steps took me after leaving it. What I shall never forget is my visit to the small settlement there, the hamlet of Mardale Green. I walked down the lane to it between stone walls draped with ivy and stained with lichens aware of an eerie stillness and absence of movement in the scene: there was no sign of human life and the cows and the sheep had gone from the fields. I came to the Dun Bull, which for two centuries had kept an open door for passing travellers, only to find it empty and unoccupied. The tiny church in its surround of yews was deserted. The few nearby cottages had been abandoned. I felt uncomfortable, a trespasser. The birds were singing and the hedgerows were fragrant with flowers and wild roses, but over all was an awful silence. It was the silence of death. The place was doomed.

At the other end of the valley men were constructing a massive dam that would convert Mardale's natural lake into a huge reservoir, the waters of which would encroach to the dalehead, submerging everything below a raised water level and drowning Mardale Green.

I climbed up to Kidsty Howes and looked down on a scene both beautiful and tragic. Sunlight dappled the pastures, lovely trees were in full leaf, but of life and movement there was none. Mardale Green was dead.

Occasionally, as in the long drought of 1984, the waters recede and the skeletal remains of the dismantled buildings return to daylight, a sight even sadder. Poor Mardale Green. It was a lovely spot, shy and secluded, happy and contented and quite undeserving of its cruel fate.

Mardale Head from Kidsty Pike

Mardale Head and Haweswater

There is a sharp descent from Kidsty Howes to the site of Riggindale Farm, another casualty of the flood, and here will be found a path that keeps to the west side of Haweswater for four miles, this path being constructed by Manchester Corporation, who created the reservoir, to compensate for the submergence of the country lane along the valley. The walking is pleasant when not impeded by high bracken. Birks Crag is passed and the old fort on its crest can be attained by a steep scramble if desired, and throughout there is always the high skyline of the High Street ridge up on the left. Looking back, a splendid view of Mardale Head is obtained although marred by the ugly tidemark of the reservoir.

After three miles of easy travel along the path, Measand is reached. Here formerly was a large house, Measand Beck Hall, and a little school, both victims of the reservoir scheme. Unaffected, however, is the series of waterfalls, known as The Forces, issuing from a gorge at this point and now crossed by a bridge. In days gone by, The Forces were a popular objective of picnic parties on half-day expeditions.

Beyond Measand, the path widens to a cart-track and the great dam comes into full view, and before it is reached the reservoir is seen to be augmented by supplies entering from the Heltondale tunnel and, across the water, by the flow from the Swindale tunnel. The dam is more than 500 yds long, has a height of 96 ft above the former river bed and impounds water with a surface area three times greater than that of the original lake. There has been a recent proposal to raise the dam even higher but this seems to be shelved for the time being. Good!

The Forces, Measand

When the dam is passed, there is a short descent to the reservoir village of Burn Banks, where the two hundred men engaged on its construction were housed in new bungalows. These remain, and Burn Banks has matured into a pleasant community amongst trees in the shelter of the dam.

Here we leave Lakeland although still within the boundary of the National Park, and a cross-country trek follows, on rights of way, in pastoral surroundings with a scattering of farmsteads, to make acquaintance with the River Lowther at Rosgill Bridge.

Above *The Haweswater Dam*

Below *Rosgill Bridge*

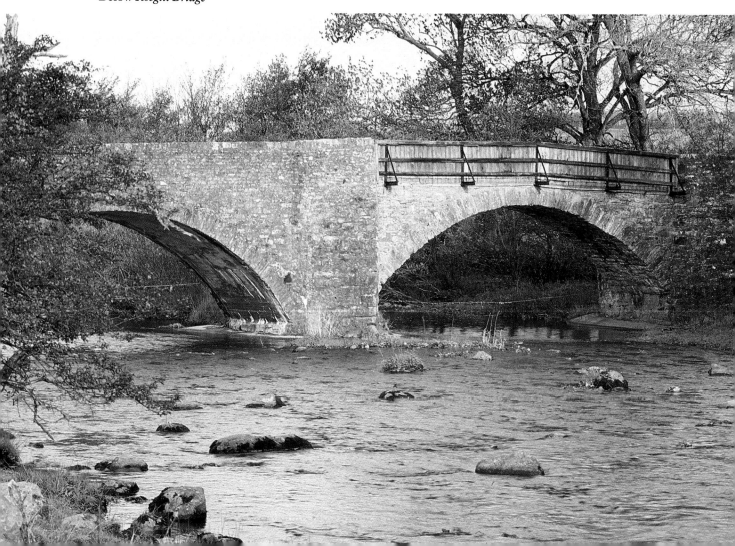

Packhorse bridge over Swindale Beck

Swindale Beck

Below *Approach to Shap Abbey*

Acquaintance with the River Lowther at Rosgill Bridge is brief, a good track south from this point being taken to come alongside a small tributary, Swindale Beck, which is crossed by a little packhorse bridge in a delightfully leafy setting, to reach a minor road at Rayside, from which a return is made to the Lowther by field paths that lead to Shap Abbey.

The history of Shap Abbey began in 1191 with the foundation near Kendal of a convent for Premonstratensian Canons, this establishment being moved to Shap in 1199 when construction of the Abbey commenced, work continued on various additions into the sixteenth century. In 1540, it was surrendered to Henry VIII and then fell into disrepair and ruin, many of the carved stones being removed to Lowther Castle. Early this century, the structure was in a sad state but happily was taken over by the Ministry of Works in 1948 and further decay has been arrested by a consolidation of all the remaining fabric, of which only the west tower retains its original height. It is preserved as an ancient monument and access by the public is permitted by the new custodians, English Heritage.

A captive sheep is given the duty of keeping the grass around the ruins cropped short, a task it performs nobly and with obvious pleasure.

Shap Abbey

From the Abbey, a road climbs a hill to join another leading into Shap village, now in sight ahead. On the final approach to the village, there is ample evidence of the limestone bedrock in the massive white walls forming the field boundaries.

But not all the stones hereabouts are limestone. In the fields are some erratics, huge boulders of unhewn granite obviously brought there and placed in their positions for a purpose.

These are the famous Shap Stones. According to early historians, they are relics of a monolithic monument of great significance: they record the existence of an avenue formed by two parallel rows of boulders 25 yds apart and extending north-west for nearly a mile from a stone circle still to be seen in an enclosure between the A.6 and the railway at the south end of the village.

The Thunder Stone, 31 feet in girth, is in a field at High Barn.

This stone has been built into the wall of a narrow lane to Keld.

This stone, in a field, is distinctly inscribed with two ring marks.

The Goggleby Stone until recently stood erect on its narrow end.

Most accessible is this stone in a field near the village on the west side.

The stone circle

Shap has been notorious amongst road travellers since stage-coach times: for many, the very name evokes vivid memories of hazardous journeys in snow and storm and mist over the A.6, the highest main road in the country, nearly 1400 ft at its summit in a moorland wilderness and having a bad accident record.

Its importance as a traffic artery to Scotland, however, was diminished at a stroke on a day in October 1970 by the opening of the M.6 motorway, this taking a lower and less exposed route. It was a red letter day for many of Shap's residents, a black letter day for others whose livelihood depended on catering for the constant stream of motorists and lorry drivers passing through; in heavy snowfalls, the village was choked with stranded vehicles. Shap became quiet overnight. Commerce suffered an immediate decline. The road was its lifeblood. Transport cafés, lodging houses, hotels and garages lost much of their trade . . . The economy of the village is now largely based on the huge granite works and limestone quarries nearby, none of them a source of beauty nor relieving the bare landscape.

The village straggles the A.6 for almost a mile but has little width. There are shops in variety, some of the cafés and boarding houses have survived, the hotels are open and there should be no difficulty in finding overnight accommodation.

Top *17th-century Market Hall, Shap*

Below *Main Street in Shap*

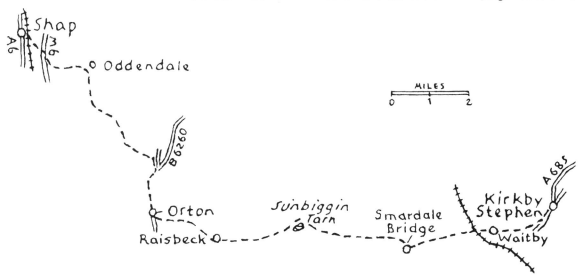

NOW THE character of the terrain changes completely. The Lake District National Park was left behind at Shap Abbey and ahead is a limestone landscape rarely visited and relatively unknown, almost a blank on the map, yet for the observant a region of immense fascination. Walkers with archaeological and antiquarian interests and students of pre-history may well consider the next twenty miles the most rewarding of all: the ancient Britons had a great liking for this part of Westmorland and left behind a display of their settlements and villages, burial mounds, stone circles and tumuli in amazing profusion.

The well-informed in relics of the past may indeed prefer to travel slowly and make leisurely explorations as they go along, breaking the journey by an overnight stay at Orton. Others more concerned with ticking off the miles will push on to the fleshpots of Kirkby Stephen, but even they will be mightily impressed by the unique quality of the natural surroundings throughout this cross-country trek.

With a rucksack replenished with goodies, Shap should be left by a side road off the A.6 opposite the King's Arms. This hotel changed its name to the Albion just after my guidebook was published, necessitating a correction, and later, to my chagrin, reverted to the King's Arms, necessitating another – an example of the frustrations suffered by guidebook writers. There is personal gratification at this point, however, the highway authorities having erected a 'Coast to Coast' signpost – official recognition at last!

The route goes through fields to a footbridge spanning the M.6, confirming the right of way, and then skirts a large limestone quarry to arrive at the shy hamlet of Oddendale.

The motorway footbridge

Oddendale is so secluded amongst its sheltering trees that it seems to have escaped the notice of the Ordnance Survey, the name being omitted from their 1″ maps. At this point, the parish of Crosby Ravensworth is entered, a parish remarkable for the numerous evidences of early British communities within its boundaries. It is clear from the profusion of ground traces that the area housed a large native population in prehistoric times: within a few miles are the remains of eleven ancient British settlements with groups of huts and enclosures defining the village precincts. These early inhabitants chose their locations well: this was open hunting country and, although they would be less concerned with environmental amenities, a most delightful place to live, their villages being in the beautiful Vale of Lyvennet, a fertile oasis in the heart of the Westmorland limestone plateau.

Today all is quiet and peaceful. The parish is entirely rural and everywhere fair to look upon, with the sequestered buildings of Crosby Ravensworth at its centre, away from the usual routes of tourists, without a fast road and a world apart from urban influences.

Without disturbing the privacy of Oddendale, a cart-track outside its walls and rising across open ground due south is followed and almost at once the first of the antiquities is seen on the right in the form of a double stone circle, one ring of stones within another. Next, a tumulus is seen on the left.

Stone circle near Oddendale

The track continues to Potrigg, named on Ordnance maps although merely a barn at the edge of a walled enclosure (modern) with a windbreak of trees, used for wintering sheep brought in from their summer grazings on the moors. Another such enclosure is seen on the left: this is rounded in a depression beyond which a stake on the top of a rise ahead is the next objective.

Before reaching the stake, which indicates another tumulus, a level grass roadway contouring the hillside is crossed unexpectedly. This is the Roman road linking their forts at Low Borrow Bridge and Brougham, having climbed over Orton Scar, and here is well preserved and recognisable.

Above *Potrigg*

Below *The Roman road on Crosby Ravensworth Fell*

The route is not defined by a path hereabouts, but from the tumulus on the crest of the hill the direction is clear, a wide view opening up of the Vale of Lyvennet, beautifully wooded and serene, and a beeline is made for the long wall of an enclosure around the headwaters of its river. On the gentle descent, a few very large and isolated boulders are passed and it will be noted that these are of red Shap granite and therefore alien to the limestone terrain around. Erratics such as these are found scattered throughout the region and others occur in distant parts of northern England, obviously the result of glacial action. Six of them in the parish of Crosby Ravensworth are named Thunder Stone and, curiously, all of them stand on the parish boundary.

The verdant landscape now stretching away to the north on both sides of the shallow basin of the River Lyvennet looks entirely pastoral, almost parklike, and from this distance shows no traces of the early villages that once were its only inhabited places. Of these the settlement of Ewe Close was the largest and most complex and is today the most renowned and deserving of inspection by historians, having clear traces of huts and walled enclosures although some parts of the site are so decayed that the detailed arrangements are no longer discernible, only the perimeter wall remaining well defined. The date of this settlement is obscure, but it is believed that the Roman road, which has disappeared under cultivation hereabouts, deviated from its straight course to avoid the settlement, this suggesting that its existence preceded the Roman occupation.

The settlements are too far from the route to warrant a detour and are, in any case, the province of the expert archaeologist, but the curious layman can be assured that other British villages will be seen at close range before the end of the day's march.

The Vale of Lyvennet

The long enclosure wall across the headwaters of the river is a perfect guide on the next stage of the journey, being accompanied by a distinct and continuous track formed by generations of sheep. Amongst the trees over the wall is another antiquity: an ancient dyke thought to have been the boundary of a former deer park.

By short detours into the bare moorland outside the wall are two other surprising discoveries. The first is found by walking up the stream bed of the infant Lyvennet, often dry, to a barren spot, all bog and heather and coarse grass, where stands an obelisk, a monument recording an event in 1651 where Charles II once halted. It is difficult to realise, but nevertheless a fact, that the first road from London to Scotland came this way across inhospitable moorland before being re-routed over Shap Fells. No trace remains. Nature has claimed her own.

The second surprise occurs further along the wall, where another dry stream bed comes down from the moor: 150 yards along this is a large cairn, indicated in ancient lettering on Ordnance maps as Robin Hood's Grave, a name not to be interpreted literally. Robin is given credence for being in many unlikely locations in the north of England.

Monument at Black Dub

This bears the following inscription:

HERE AT BLACK DUB
THE SOURCE OF THE LIVENNET
KING CHARLES THE II
REGALED HIS ARMY
AND DRANK OF THE WATER
ON HIS MARCH FROM SCOTLAND
AUGUST 8 1651

The obelisk was erected in 1843

Robin Hood's Grave

The wall is then followed to its end at a minor road serving the village of Crosby Ravensworth, arriving opposite a large quarry still in operation. A short walk to the right leads to its junction with the B.6260 (Kendal—Appleby) on the edge of Orton Scar.

Orton Scar before . . .

Orton Scar is an upland area of limestone, a delightful place to explore, the surface outcrops and extensive pavements of white rocks appearing on the ground weathered by frost and rain and wind, and fretted into attractive and often grotesque shapes. But it has become a place of appalling permitted vandalism. Since the war, to satisfy a demand for garden and rockery ornaments, large tracts of the Scar have been stripped of surface stones, cruelly hacked out of the ground, leaving devastated areas scattered with chippings and rutted by the lorries that carry loads away for sale to garden enthusiasts. These areas will never recover. Operations of this sort, greatly to be deplored, need planning permission, and it is amazing that the planners, the guardians of the environment, have permitted this desecration of an attractive natural landscape. It is a practice that should never have been allowed and should be stopped. It is vandalism with official blessing.

. . . and Orton Scar after

From the road junction onwards for the next few miles, my planned route later went adrift. Originally it went up alongside a wall to the beacon on Orton Scar, a magnificent viewpoint, using a path often trodden by visitors to the monument there, and then continued on a rough beeline aiming for Sunbiggin Tarn, first crossing a depression by gates in enclosures and then climbing slightly to the high limestone wall around Great Asby Scar. My primary object here was to visit that most spectacular of ancient British settlements, Castle Folds, which I knew was sited on the other side of the wall. But surprisingly, I could not find a stile that would give access to it although I paced the wall for hundreds of yards in search of one, and finally had to resort to scaling it at a point where a junction of walls seemed to offer a crossing. I hate climbing high drystone walls: there is always a danger of immediate collapse, but there was little difficulty, others clearly having preceded me, presumably archaeologists visiting the settlement.

Jubilee Monument (1887)
Beacon Hill, Orton Scar

I found myself on the edge of the largest limestone pavement I had ever seen, a vast sheet of naked rock level to walk on but criss-crossed by a mosaic of fissures and little crevices and, in its midst, a low ridge rising from it like an island springing from a sea and carrying the decayed walls of the settlement. Castle Folds is remarkable: a sight all should see. Then I followed the ridge through a wilderness of limestone outcrops, to a lane promised by the map, finding a gate across it so heavily barricaded by barbed wire and corrugated iron that it could not be opened, and again I had to search for a weakness in the adjoining wall to gain access to the lane, which then took me very pleasantly down to Sunbiggin Tarn.

I had no doubt that there was no right of way across the scar and that I had trespassed on private land, but relied on the general acceptance by northern landowners of open access over high uncultivated land, as obtains in Lakeland and the Pennines and the Yorkshire moors.

However, I was soon to be disillusioned. A year or so after my guidebook was published, incorporating this section, I was taken to task by the farmer for encouraging walkers to enter upon his private land. I saw him and thought I had placated him, but after an interval he renewed his complaint, saying that he had found campers on his land and had introduced a bull to the route, and this time was supported by a protest from the Country Landowners' Association. Under such pressure, I had to agree to amend the route, which I did with many fervent damns and blasts. Anyone who wants to see Castle Folds must first get the farmer's permission to do so.

The only alternative way to Sunbiggin Tarn is by walking along the tarmac roads, always to be avoided if possible, and I revised the route accordingly. Happily, the roads in these parts are quiet, being more in the nature of country lanes, and progress along them is fast and relatively traffic-free. The revised route has one compensation: it includes a visit to Orton, one of the prettiest of Westmorland villages, with a hotel and a few shops.

The road down to Orton from the junction on the crest of the Scar passes immediately from wild moorland to pastoral loveliness, and at once, opposite a disused quarry used as a car park by visitors to the beacon, there is a glorious prospect of the upper Lune valley backed by the Howgill Fells.

The upper Lune valley from Orton Scar

The road descends steeply and at the foot of the hill, the first habitations since leaving Oddendale are reached. Beyond, on the left before entering Orton, is a splendid example of a restored farmhouse that, some fifteen years ago, was unoccupied, partly derelict and stripped of its antique fittings. It was offered for sale at £1100 with extensive outbuildings, a barn and a private woodland, and for a long time there were no takers but eventually a buyer was found who, to his credit, repaired, restored and refurbished the property, converting it into a most attractive residence. Such conversions of old buildings have been commonplace in northern districts since the war, the work invariably being undertaken with care and a sensitive regard to the environment. It is sad to see an old farmhouse abandoned, sadder still to see one falling into ruin, and those who come along to bring them back to life are to be applauded.

Bow Brow
Below *View of Lakeland from near Orton Scar*

Then comes Orton, embowered in lovely trees and heralded by the fine tower of its church. This is a charming village, built around a field that serves as the village green between two streams crossed by many miniature bridges. There are terraces of old cottages, tidily kept, a few handsome houses and a farmhouse that was formerly a manor house, and has the date 1604 over its doorway. A haven for retirement!

Two scenes in Orton

Orton is left along the road heading east past the grounds of Orton Hall, now let in flats. A lane going off to the left at a bend in the road has, over a wall on the right, a circle of thirty-six stones about 50 yds in diameter and known locally as the Druidical Temple. A curious feature is the exclusive selection of erratic boulders of Shap granite, the native limestone bedrock being ignored.

The road is continued to the hamlet of Raisbeck, where a branch to the left signposted 'Sunbiggin' is ignored (this leads only to the farm of that name) in favour of another just beyond that gives a pleasant two-mile walk to Sunbiggin Tarn, the approach to it being heralded at nesting time by a cacophony of sound emanating from hundreds of screaming gulls long before the tarn comes into sight.

Stone circle, Orton
Below *Sunbiggin Tarn*

Sunbiggin Tarn has no pretensions to beauty; its appearance is that of a large reedy pond in the middle of a morass difficult to negotiate. The attractions of this desolate place lie in other directions: it is the haunt and nesting place of many varying water fowl, a rewarding 'station' for bird-watchers. Botanists too find delight in the profuse display of the delicate and lovely bird's-eye primrose, rampant on the roadside banks in this area. Geologists will seek to find a reason for the existence of so large a sheet of water in surroundings so dominated by limestone cliffs and outcrops known to be porous and unable to contain static water, and discover the answer just below the road where the limestone ends abruptly along a line of many bubbling springs, the tarn itself, of course, occupies a base of impermeable rock.

Beyond the tarn, the route departs from the road near a major spring and crosses a marshy flat to a stile that gives access to the heathery expanse of Rayseat Pike, its cairn reached by a slight ascent. Clearly seen nearby is an ancient monument regarded as perhaps the most important relic of its kind surviving. It is a long barrow or burial mound and appears as the stony crest of a small green hill. This is thought to be the earliest evidence of the pre-history of the region. Excavated and measured in 1875, the search revealed the remains of both adults and children. An unexpected discovery was a cremation trench containing many burnt bones, a feature that has caused speculation about the age of this ancient burial ground. The dimensions of the barrow were ascertained as 179 ft in length with a width tapering from 62 ft to 36 ft.

Rayseat Pike long barrow

Through thick heather, a rough crossing is next made to a minor road, reached at a cattle grid, and a rising path opposite is followed alongside a wall, soon becoming a high-level traverse along the lower slope of Crosby Garrett Fell with splendid views of Mallerstang Edge, Wild Boar Fell and the Howgill Fells. Also worthy of admiring attention are the drystone walls hereabouts, excellently constructed and monuments to the forgotten men who built them two centuries ago.

Still accompanying the intake wall, the solitary outpost of Bents Farm is passed.

A drystone wall near Bents Farm
Below *Path on Crosby Garrett Fell*

Soon after passing Bents Farm, a gate in the wall gives private access to a large enclosure in which is the prehistoric British village promised earlier. Half a mile further along the wall is the official entrance to the site and it is a matter of conscience which is used.

This village settlement is known as Severals and is extraordinary, something very special, an education in living conditions thousands of years ago. The Royal Commission on Ancient Monuments in their inventory of Westmorland describe Severals as a key site and one of the most remarkable in Britain: a complex of stone-walled fields, hutments, dykes and pathways extending over a considerable area. The remains are fragmentary and a trained eye and a learned mind are attributes necessary to piece together the story of these

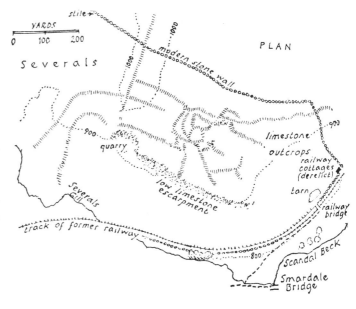

primitive ruins and earthworks: the parapets are the foundations of former boundaries and enclosures, the sunken ways were farm tracks and the small patterned sections are the traces of stone huts.

Men lived here as a community where no men now live and few men today ever come. A gap in our knowledge of the early settlers in the district might well be bridged by expert excavation of the site.

Smardale Bridge

The principal settlement, Severals, covers three acres; there are two others immediately to the north, the whole area of occupation extending over an area of 100 acres.

A modern wall divides the settlements and a stile in it is used to pass through the main site on a descending slope to a disused railway track, which is crossed to reach Smardale Bridge in a lovely unfrequented valley containing other prehistoric remains, these of a different type but possibly once associated with life at Severals.

Upstream from Smardale Bridge in a sloping field on the right are some raised mounds, rectangular in plan, about 15 yds long and 5 yds wide, and obviously not natural formations. They are indicated on Ordnance maps as Giants' Graves, the name attributed to them by local informants at the time of the first survey; their origin, however, was and is still not known.

The purpose of these 'pillow mounds' is still obscure, the only certain thing being that they are not the graves of giants. Similar ancient mounds in other parts of the country have been identified as warrens made by man to facilitate the breeding and capture of rabbits, but here in Smardale this explanation is unlikely to apply, for their proximity to the old settlements strongly suggests an association with the early Britons: rabbits were not introduced into this country until after the 11th century, but the settlements and the mounds almost certainly date back to the dawn of history. The mounds have the appearance of long barrows or burial sites, but this possibility is discounted by the best authorities, who seem more prepared to accept the theory, pending verification, that they may well have been built as platforms for stacking bracken.

There is a field of inquiry waiting near Smardale Bridge for an archaeologist with a spade.

Giants' Graves, Smardale

The delightful valley of Smardale, lovely in its shy seclusion, is little known outside the immediate locality yet has a quiet and sylvan charm not found in places favoured by tourists. It cannot be described as unspoilt because a railway formerly threaded a curving passage through it and has left abandoned railway cottages and a mill, but it did not, and does not, detract from the beauty of the scene; indeed the high graceful viaduct spanning Smardale Beck is a spectacular highlight. This was the most attractive stretch of the old Tebay—Darlington line, and its dismantled track today gives pleasure to botanists, the flowery banks being the habitat of plants not commonly seen, notably the bloody cranesbill, while the trackway over the viaduct is a carpet of roseroot. At the head of the valley, in the midst of woodland, the more famous Settle—Carlisle line crosses overhead.

If time permits, a short detour up the valley, at least as far as the viaduct, will amply repay the time taken.

The railway viaduct, Smardale

The walk continues from Smardale Bridge along a cart-track rising above the Giants' Graves to the open moorland of Smardale Fell, passing a curious mile-long but very narrow walled enclosure and topping a rise with a commanding view ahead of Nine Standards and the long line of the Pennines across the Eden Valley – the next stage of the journey. This elevation is known as Limekiln Hill, appropriatcly, for on the descent from it two limekilns are passed, the first in near-perfect condition, the second ruinous. These kilns are a not unusual feature of the northern limestone districts and have a common pattern, each having a hearth in which limestone dropped through a hole in the roof was burnt to produce lime for sweetening the pastures. All are now disused. Agricultural lime now comes to the farms in bags: much less trouble!

A minor road to Waitby is reached but soon left for a path passing under the Settle—Carlisle railway to enter a field where are the remains of two more settlements, the first adjoining the railway, the second cut into two by the line, parts being seen on both sides of the embankment.

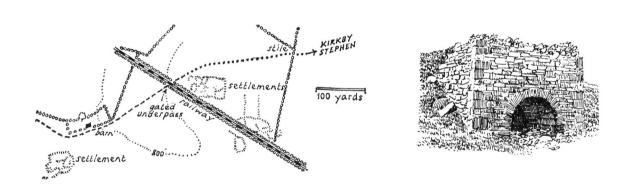

Kirkby Stephen is now close ahead and field paths and lanes lead into the outskirts, again crossing the disused Tebay—Darlington railway. Even here on the fringe of the town, the ancient monuments persist, for on the crest of a green hill in suburbia is Croglam Castle, a name belied by its appearance, the site having merely a rampart and a ditch. Nevertheless, it was a primitive fort, probably pallisaded, and although never excavated for confirmation is thought to have been one of many hill forts used by tribes of Brigantes before the coming of the Romans.

Thus ends a wonderful day's walk, a journey of engrossing fascination especially for those with an interest in things long past. Since leaving Shap there has been a succession of prehistoric relics and the mind has been absorbed by the many more evidences of the way of life of forgotten ancestors. It has been a walk three thousand years back in time. It has been a day of ancient monuments.

Then, in a few paces, the fantasy ends abruptly as the busy main street of Kirkby Stephen is entered amidst the noise of traffic, the bright lights and shops of a modern civilisation. The people on the pavements are twentieth-century Britons.

Kirkby Stephen is an old market town of pre-Norman origin and the commercial centre of a wide agricultural area. A perambulation of the main thoroughfare gives the impression that the town is larger than it really is, being tightly built up for almost a mile, but it has little width, the River Eden forming a close boundary on the east side and hill pastures flanking it on the west. Interest is centred mainly around the market place, which has a picturesque grouping of buildings in many individual styles overlooked by the venerable old church. The market has had a charter since 1351, but the greatest volume of trade is conducted in the auction marts. There is a grammar school in new premises but founded in 1596, several institutions for social, educational and recreational pursuits, places of worship for religious denominations in variety, and a public hall. Not long ago, the town enjoyed the luxury of two railway stations, both inconveniently situated at high levels: the nearer one has been closed but a train journey on the spectacular but threatened Settle—Carlisle line can still be enjoyed. The main road through the town is the A.685 connecting Kendal and Brough.

Coast to Coast walkers will be primarily interested in the catering facilities. There are shops and cafés galore, a multiplicity of fish and chip shops (one of them bearing the name 'Coast to Coast'), many hotels and boarding houses and a Youth Hostel.

For the information of visitors to the parish church of St Stephen, a notice inside tells the story of the three churches that have stood on this site: first a Saxon church, probably of timber, followed in 1170 by a Norman church, which in turn was replaced in 1240 by the present structure, itself altered and enlarged on subsequent occasions.

This is a large church, second in size in Westmorland to that at Kendal, the internal proportions being impressive. Many Saxon stones are on view in the nave, and the thirteenth-century arcades and elaborate pulpit of polished granite and marble are features of unusual interest.

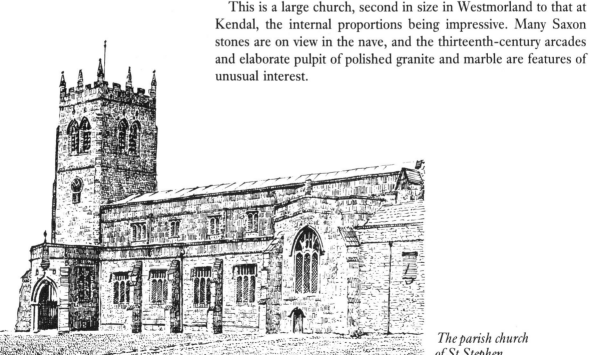

*The parish church
of St Stephen*

Street scenes in Kirkby Stephen

The church environs, Kirkby Stephen

Frank's Bridge

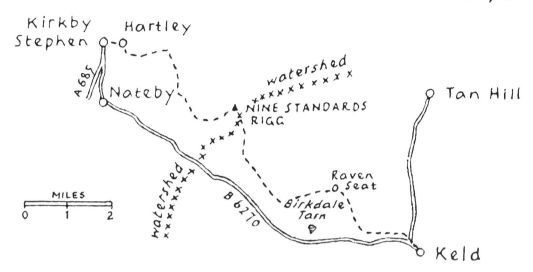

KIRKBY STEPHEN to KELD: $12\frac{3}{4}$ miles

THREE important milestones on the journey are passed in the section from Kirkby Stephen. The Yorkshire Dales National Park is entered, the main watershed of the Pennines is crossed and at Keld the halfway stage of the walk is reached.

Parts of the terrain are pathless and rough. In mist, there could be difficulty in following the route and a danger of going seriously astray, but it would be a pity to miss the memorable crossing of Nine Standards because of horrid conditions. But if lack of available time will not allow a longer stay in Kirkby until they improve or if an advance booking of accommodation at Keld has already been made, the sensible course of action would be to take the moorland road from Kirkby via Nateby to Keld and so avoid problems and doubts.

Appetites should be fully satisfied and rucksacks fully stocked before departing from Kirkby Stephen. No other opportunities for replenishing either will occur along the way and supplies at Keld are chancy.

The first objective is the village of Hartley, half a mile away and reached through fields from the picturesque Frank's Bridge over the River Eden, a short lane leading to it from the market place.

Looking back to Kirkby Stephen

Hartley is a delightful backwater, a small village lining a no-through road and spared the intrusions of tourists. Buildings of distinctive character face the road on both sides across a lovely stream flowing under a canopy of mature trees. The cottage gardens are bright with flowers and maintained with pride: in springtime, there are daffodils everywhere. Hartley is a good example of the charm that results from haphazard arrangement without the help of planning experts. There is one source of disturbance: the heavy lorries that shuttle to and from a huge quarry on the nearby fellside.

Hartley

It was at Hartley that I transgressed again when planning the route. The farm at the top end of the village (occupying the site of a medieval building and named Hartley Castle) is the start of a cart-track that winds pleasantly through fields and rises to meet an access road to a hill farm, Ladthwaite, where a friendly farmer assured me that there would be no objection to the use of this route. The farmer at Hartley Castle, however, protested after my guidebook had been published and a solicitor's letter left me in no doubt that there was no public right of way through the fields. Consequently I had to amend the route, which now keeps along the road past the quarry, climbing steadily to another farm, Fell House, then becoming the access road to Ladthwaite.

Hartley Quarry

It is from this access road that the long climb to Nine Standards commences, a signpost pointing the way along a distinct and well-graded cart-track leading to old coal pits at an elevation of 2000 ft; without the help of this engineered way, the ascent would be arduous, the terrain being rough and wild.

During the walk up to the old coal pits, Faraday Gill opens straight ahead and invites a direct climb to the skyline of Nine Standards, but the invitation should be declined and the more circuitous and much easier cart-track kept underfoot. Soon there comes into view the deep ravine of Rigg Beck on the right: this is a favourite haunt of botanists and, on the limestone plateau at its head, of potholers.

Then the old pits are reached, the cart-track ends, and directly in front is the long skyline of Nine Standards Rigg.

The left extremity of the ridge is the next aim and after a short climb, the ground levels out to reveal the remarkable array of cairns long known as the Nine Standards.

Faraday Gill

Nine Standards

In the absence of historical fact, there are different theories about the origin of the nine large cairns so conspicuously sited on the Pennine watershed between the valleys of the rivers Eden and Swale. They are certainly old, appearing as the Nine Standards on eighteenth-century maps and giving their name to the hilltop they adorn. They have multiplied in number, modern visitors having added a few more of lesser stature to the collection. One romantic suggestion is that they were built to give marauding Scots advancing up the Eden valley the false impression that an English army was encamped here. More likely is that they were boundary markers (the county boundary formerly passed through them) or beacons. Harder to believe is that the builders were local lads with nothing better to do to pass the time. Whatever the purpose, the cairns were meant to endure and have suffered little from the storms of centuries.

View west from Nine Standards Rigg

Walking south from the Nine Standards along the crest of the ridge, the highest point of the fell is reached at an Ordnance column standing at 2178 ft. Arrival here is an occasion for celebration: at this precise point, the Pennine watershed is attained and east takes the place of west in the minds of Coast to Coast walkers. No longer will all streams make their way west to the Irish Sea; from now on, all are destined to flow east to the North Sea.

As a viewpoint, Nine Standards Rigg excels. Here, if visibility is clear, is the most extensive panorama that will be seen on the walk. In the west is a farewell sighting of the Lakeland skyline; Cross Fell and Mickle Fell form the northern horizon beyond the wilderness of Stainmore, overlooking many miles of the Eden Valley; south, nearer, are the Mallerstang heights, and eastwards between the portals of Rogan's Seat and Great Shunner Fell stretches the lovely valley of Swaledale, its further reaches lost in the haze of distance. It is to the latter direction that most eyes will turn: there is the territory next to be traversed, and it is a prospect that pleases. Somewhere in the distant haze is the foot of the rainbow for Coast to Coast walkers: journey's end.

Millstones

The walk continues south, now in the Yorkshire Dales National Park, without the help of a path, and aims for the grassy top of White Mossy Hill which has a modest cairn of two stones only. Birkdale Tarn comes into sight here and sets the direction for further progress: this large sheet of water, artificially dammed, was formerly used to provide supplies for lead mining operations around Swaledale. The next objective, reached by a long and exhilarating descent at an easy gradient, is a conspicuous stone pillar in an area of gritstone outcrops known as Millstones. Down on the right on a parallel course is the deep valley of Birkdale, carrying the road between Nateby and Keld. Then, in a depression, a rutted path appears: this, if followed to the right, joins the road and is a valuable time-saver. But the planned route turns left, in the direction of flow of Ney Gill and with the stream alongside enters Whitsundale amid a scattering of shooting butts.

The valley of Whitsundale bisects an upland wilderness east of Nine Standards Rigg and winds down into the lower reaches of Birkdale. It drains an area of considerable extent yet is little known and rarely visited: deeply enclosed by barren moors, it is unseen from usual pedestrian tracks and unsuspected from the only motor road in the vicinity. A few farms occupy the entrance to the valley but beyond the tiny farming community of Raven Seat, linked to civilisation by a slender strip of tarmac, all is desolation profound.

Raven Seat

Ney Gill joins forces with Whitsundale Beck but before the confluence is forded to reach the narrow road that serves as Raven Seat's lifeline. This lonely outpost, comprising a sheep farm and a few cottages, is skirted to get access to a gated cart-track on the east bank of Whitsundale Beck, and this, with the beck as a lively companion, proceeds south to meet the River Swale. On the way, the stream enters a deep ravine that rejoices in the name of Boggle Hole: there are dramatic glimpses into its depth from the wall along its edge.

Whitsundale Beck

Below *Boggle Hole*

Beyond Boggle Hole, the path becomes indistinct as it contours an open fellside, passing a sheepfold that deserves an Oscar award as the largest ever seen, and two farmhouses, the first unoccupied, a cart-track then appearing and descending as a lane to the River Swale, a waterway of recurring delights, where the road from Nateby is joined over a bridge. A turn left alongside the river soon brings into view the first of Keld's waterfalls, Wain Wath Force, in a spectacular setting below a wooded limestone cliff.

Keld is half a mile further along the road.

Wain Wath Force

Arrival at Keld is a memorable occasion. Half of the journey has now been accomplished.

Keld is the first village in Swaledale, a welcome oasis encompassed by bleak moorlands, a friendly refuge in an unfriendly landscape. It is small, its stone buildings straggling its only street in an haphazard yet tidy arrangement, many of them, even the chapel belfry, bearing proud dates and the names of proud men. A large sundial proclaims the hours but time here is measured in centuries, Keld being an ancient settlement of Scandinavian origin: its name is a Norse word meaning 'a place by the river', and there has been little change for many generations. It is attractively situated on a 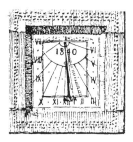 headland above the Swale, the river rushing past in a series of impressive waterfalls and cascades, of which Catrake Force and Kisdon Force, each in a lovely wooded setting, are the best known. Everybody loves Keld, and the Swale, a sparkling torrent, is its special joy.

Overnight accommodation is limited. The former Cathole Inn, with a reputation for hospitality, has closed; there is a Youth Hostel, converted from a shooting lodge, and a few cottages cater for visitors. If lodgings here have not been booked in advance, it is advisable to arrive in good time, otherwise it might be necessary to go on to the next villages of Thwaite and Muker in search of a bed.

Keld   Overleaf *Kisdon Force*

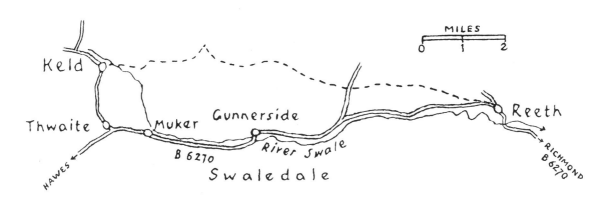

MILES
0   1   2

BETWEEN Keld and Reeth lies an upland desert formerly comprehensively exploited for lead mining operations, and the route has been designed to pass through the heart of the old workings. No scenes of beauty are promised and none will be seen: this is a grim trek amidst the debris of a dead industry, amidst the skeletons of a past enterprise that once flourished exceedingly and then, in the space of a few years, withered and was abandoned. It is an unforgettable experience to see the stark environment in which thousands of men laboured up to a century ago, and walkers with an interest in industrial archaeology especially will be fascinated by this excursion back in time to a graveyard and its ghosts. The scene is one of utter man-made devastation stripped of all natural beauty. This day will be remembered as the day of the lead mines.

This, however, is another section better undertaken under a favourable sky. In mist, the route will be difficult to follow through a maze of miners' tracks and sledgates and reliance must be placed on a compass to keep on an easterly course.

Footbridge at Keld

In bad weather conditions, it is advisable instead to stay in the company of the Swale, by country roads and riverside paths all the way to Reeth: this is the royal way to see Swaledale, a journey of supreme delight.

Exit from Keld is made along a muddy lane to a Pennine Way sign pointing to a footbridge over the Swale, and for five minutes the two routes coincide, crossing the river and ascending the slope beyond alongside another waterfall, East Gill Force.

East Gill Force

Below *The ruins of Crackpot Hall*

Above East Gill Force, the many travel-stained hikers who come up from the bridge follow their chosen course – Pennine Wayfarers turning left for Tan Hill and Coast to Coast walkers turning right to cross the stream and enter a cart-track that rises gently above the wooded valley of the Swale and arrives at the decaying ruin of Crackpot Hall. All ruins are sad because of the memories associated with them. Crackpot Hall is especially forlorn: this once handsome residence occupies an enviable site overlooking a lovely stretch of the river.

The valley of the Swale from Crackpot Hall

A good track continues behind Crackpot Hall. There is a last retrospective view of Keld and then the scenery changes suddenly as the deep rift of Swinner Gill is reached, its stream scurrying down to the greenery of Swaledale as though glad to escape from the arid surroundings of its source. The track turns left alongside to the head of the gill.

Lead mining country is here reached, and a new world entered.

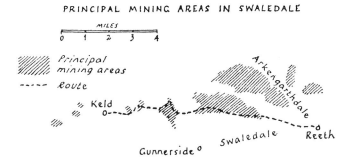

PRINCIPAL MINING AREAS IN SWALEDALE

MILES
0 1 2 3 4

▨▨ Principal
mining areas
----- Route
" Keld
Arkengarthdale
Gunnerside ∘
Swaledale   Reeth

This diagram indicates roughly the main areas extensively mined for lead, but in addition countless old shafts and levels, many of which proved abortive and were not fully developed, occur everywhere on the moors. The triangle of high ground between Arkengarthdale and Swaledale proved the most productive area, several square miles here being intensively worked — as is testified by today's sad scenery.

In a search for information relating to the happenings of centuries ago, one must often rely on imagination to fill in the details from the scanty evidences still remaining.

Not so in the case of the Swaledale lead mines. Anyone who wanders up on the moors from the valley is soon in the midst of a graphic scene of industrial decay that simply cannot be passed unnoticed. The ravines carved by streams have been further torn asunder by man, as have the hillsides and even the summits; the ground is pierced and pockmarked by shafts and levels; petrified rivers of stones litter the steep slopes; barren gullies make ugly scars in the heather; the skeletons of abandoned and derelict buildings stand gaunt and grey amid a chaos of debris and spoil heaps. An observer of this dismal wreckage is left in no doubt that Swaledale has a very long history of mining – and that this history has come to a full stop.

The date of the mines is uncertain. Most of them were opened in the seventeenth and eighteenth centuries, but it is known that the Romans extracted lead here, probably from mines already existing, and that the Yorkshire monasteries owned workings later; a free-for-all developed, the landowners and men individually and in groups plundering the moors in search of profitable veins of ore. Another Klondyke arose in these wild hills. Thousands of men were engaged: a few 'struck it rich' but most toiled for little reward. Then, in the space of a decade towards the end of the nineteenth century, the industry collapsed. Not only were the best veins exhausted but cheaper foreign imports supplied the home demand. The population of Swaledale fell dramatically. Lead mining gave way to farming as the valley's main source of prosperity.

In the triangle of land between Swaledale and Arkengarthdale particularly, the scene today is of sterile devastation, decay and despoliation. There is no beauty in these unsightly remains but a great fascination for those of imagination who can picture in their minds the scene as it was a century before, and still more for those who have the knowledge to piece together the fragments that remain.

East Grain, Swinner Gill

Swinnergill Lead Mines are the first reached on the journey and the surroundings are impressive, perhaps more so because of the silence that shrouds the scene, the silence of death. The track goes on to a bridge over the stream and all around are the typical remains of mining operations: on the far bank are the ruins of a smelt mill and the adit of a mine level is seen adjacent to a waterfall on a tributary stream coming down from a side valley, East Grain. Above the bridge, Swinner Gill threads a stony passage between the cliffs known as Swinnergill Kirk. The atmosphere is grim and rather eerie. It is now obvious that the only escape from this lifeless amphitheatre is by way of the cart-track from Keld, along which supplies and products must have been conveyed.

The bridge, Swinnergill Mines

Swinnergill Kirk   Below *Waterfall and mine level of East Grain*

The pedestrian escape from Swinnergill Mines lies up the branch valley of East Grain, where a thin track roughly ascends the north bank of the descending stream and reaches a moorland plateau at 1800 ft, the view forward opening up to give a stimulus to progress, welcome after the dreary confines of East Grain.

From the top of East Grain, there is a simple high-level traverse due east, the path becoming indistinct on wet ground until a shooting hut is reached when it becomes double-rutted and easy to follow. At the highest point of this moorland crossing, a sheet of water divided by a causeway is glimpsed distantly on the right: this is Moss Dam, an interesting relic of past days formerly used as a source of supply for the mines. As the track starts to descend, a view of the great trench of Gunnerside Gill opens in front and large areas of mining debris are reached, notably the man-engineered ravine of North Hush plunging down to the floor of the gill. The route now inclines half-left, departing from the good track, to reach the stony recesses at the head of Gunnerside Gill.

Gunnerside Gill

Blakethwaite Smelt Mill

A century ago, the deeply inurned head of Gunnerside Gill was a scene of intense mining activity and although now a place of deathly quiet, with only the stream showing movement, it is easy to imagine from the many evidences remaining, the animation and noise that once prevailed here and understand the methods of operation. The stream is crossed by a slab to the imposing ruins of the Blakethwaite Smelt Mill where the ore was processed, a fine building even in decay, with an arched entrance and an interior reminiscent of a cathedral cloister, at the foot of a steep hillside down which, straight as a die, a flue descends from a notch in the skyline high above. There are kilns and adits to be seen in disturbed ground littered with stones and rubble. This is a tortured landscape, appearing as if bombed on a massive scale, yet the ravages were done by men working with bare hands and primitive tools. The picture is without any vestige of beauty, yet will remain in mind as one of the highlights of the journey, a memory that will live.

A good path above the smelt mill leads down the gill through stony wastes intersected by hushes, the route entering the last of these, Bunton Hush, and climbing steadily upwards past a fractured cliff. Looking back, the full length of North Hush is seen directly opposite across the gill.

Hushing was the name given by miners to a practice designed to reveal veins of lead beneath the surface covering of the ground. A hush, in mining terms, is a shallow ravine contrived by prospectors on a steep slope and caused by the sudden release of water from streams dammed above in such force that the surface vegetation is stripped and the subsoil scoured with the object of revealing any mineral content that might indicate the presence of a vein. Today, a bulldozer would be used.

North Hush as seen from Bunton Hush

On emerging at the top of Bunton Hush, an open moorland plateau stretches ahead and is crossed due east with a broken wall as a guide until a good track coming up from Gunnerside is joined. Then a surprising tract of land is entered: for a third of a mile, the ground is entirely covered by gravel from the spoil heaps of the mines in the vicinity. Not a blade of grass nor a sprig of heather is visible in a vast desert of stones. The spoil here is being reclaimed and, incongruously, tractors may be seen at work. Although the altitude here exceeds 1800 ft, nothing less like a Yorkshire moor can be imagined.

The moorland crossing from Bunton Hush

This transformation of a heather moor into an arid waste may be deplored but resulting from it is one advantage for walkers: an access road has been roughly constructed for the tractors and is a great boon for travellers on foot, who can make rapid progress along it with no problems of route finding into the valley directly ahead, descending to cross a bridge and, with a stream now alongside, arrive at the stark ruin of the Old Gang Smelt Mill, another melancholy reminder of past glories. Now 100 miles of the journey have been travelled.

Lead mine

There is an urgent need, before everything crumbles into dust, to preserve at least one of the Swaledale lead mines as a site museum, not necessarily restoring the smelting and crushing mills and opening up the levels, but reclaiming enough to demonstrate the methods of operation and the tools and equipment used, with a plan of the workings, graphs of annual output and such supporting documentary records as may still be available. This could perhaps be undertaken by one of the universities or archaeological groups and should be financed from Government funds.

We have lost too much of the past through concern for the present.

Old Gang Mine

A mile of easy walking along the access road from the Old Gang ruins leads to Surrender Bridge, where the stream is crossed by an unenclosed moorland road familiar to television viewers of the original Herriot series, *All Creatures Great and Small*. Downstream from the bridge are the ruins of another smelt mill, the last industrial relic of the day's walk. A short climb up the heather slope from the ruins brings the steep-sided ravine of Cringley Bottom into view, and this is crossed by the use of narrow squeeze stiles that may cause problems for walkers with bow legs, after which a good track contours a hillside high above the stream before descending to a farm, the first habitation seen since leaving Keld, and then proceeding by field paths and lanes to enter the village of Reeth.

Reeth is a large village set around a spacious open green. It is always a welcome halting place and, as capital of mid-Swaledale, offers visitors a choice of hotels, boarding houses and shops and, a mile away at Grinton, a Youth Hostel. It occupies a strategic situation where the long side-valley of Arkengarthdale joins Swaledale and their waters mingle. Here too there is access to the next main valley, Wensleydale, by a moorland road. The road passing through Reeth, the B.6270, carries a bus service to Richmond.

A perambulation of the village discloses many interesting and picturesque nooks and corners. Altogether a pleasant place for an overnight stay.

Reeth

Village scenes in Reeth

Above *Marrick Priory*
Left *Ruins at Marrick Priory*

Marrick Priory was established in the twelfth century and occupied by Benedictine nuns until it was dissolved by Henry VIII, after which it became a ruin except for the tower. Restoration of the nave took place last century and new buildings have been added more recently, the Priory having been adapted as a residential adventure centre for young people of the Ripon Diocese.

Ruins of original buildings are still to be seen in the east corner of the site.

From the Priory, a path slants up the facing slope to a wicket gate giving entrance to a wood, where a flagged path rises in a series of rough steps between floriferous banks: a delightful interlude. The steps are reputed to be 375 in number although many are insignificant, and are locally known as the Nunnery Steps from a belief that the nuns took their exercise here.

At the top, a lane passes between a chapel and a church that give an exaggerated impression of the religious fervour of the village of Marrick beyond.

Left *Nunnery Steps*
Below *Marrick village*

The two miles onwards from Marrick lie through a succession of fields where the right of way is often invisible underfoot but indicated by gates and stiles. On a hilltop ahead, a prominent obelisk, 60 ft high, gives approximate direction in the early stages of the march: this is Hutton's Monument, marking the grave of a Matthew Hutton (1814). Of interest on the way is an outstanding example of the conversion of an old farmhouse into a modern residence. This is Ellers, and a footbridge across the beck behind points the way through more farmlands and across the former deer park of Marske Hall. The Reeth—Marske road is joined on a descent in beautiful surroundings to the wooded valley of Marske Beck and the charming village of Marske up the hill beyond.

Marske is snugly sequestered amongst handsome trees in a side valley of Swaledale, a glacial fold in the hills fringed by limestone cliffs with wild heathery moors beyond. The charm of the place is its natural scenery, the lovely grounds of Marske Hall contributing to the richness of the landscape. The Hall was for centuries the home of the distinguished Hutton family, providing two Archbishops of York, but is now occupied as flats following a sale of the estate. Also worthy of mention is the twelfth-century church of St Edmund, retaining some of the original features and fabric.

Left *Marske Beck*
Below *Marske Bridge*

Marske Church

Below *Marske Hall*

Top *Clapgate Beck*

Below *West Applegate*

The Richmond road out of Marske is followed to a gate giving access to a public but invisible path that leads to the pretty dell of Clapgate Beck, crossed by a footbridge, after which a steep slope is mounted to a farm access road. The scenery now is rich in variety and interest and of high quality: above on the left is the limestone cliff of Applegarth Scar and in a deep trench below on the right the wooded valley of the Swale, these extremes of landscape continuing as the walk proceeds along a shelf on the hillside. It is a delightful traverse suspended midway between a long limestone escarpment and a canopy of foliage shrouding the river. West Applegarth Farm is passed and East Applegarth beyond; then, looking up to the skyline, Willance's Leap is seen.

Willance's Leap is distinguished by a monument. It is not a spectacular precipice, as the name might suggest, and would attract no attention were it not associated with an occurrence in 1606 when Robert Willance fell down the steep slope here while riding. His horse was killed but Robert was unharmed and, grateful for his deliverance, gave to the town of Richmond as a thanks offering a silver chalice, preserved to this day as one of the town's treasures.

The escarpment here is Whitcliffe Scar and below it is Whitcliffe Wood, both being popular local walks. The wood is next entered and provides an enchanting walk through an avenue of mature trees bordering a farm road for almost a mile, and every step is a paradise. Compare Whitcliffe Wood with Ennerdale Forest!

Right *Whitcliffe Wood*

Below *Willance's Leap*

RICHMOND

Map of town centre and features of interest

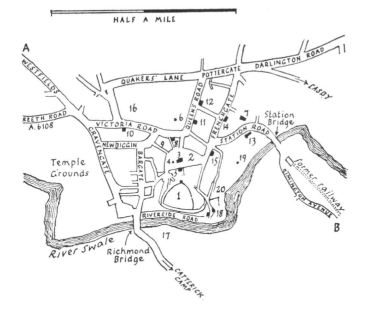

HALF A MILE

1: Castle Ruins
2: Market Place
3: Holy Trinity Church
4: Market Cross
5: Town Hall
6: Grey Friars' Tower
7: St. Mary's Parish Church
8: Georgian Theatre
9: Finkle Street
10: Cinema
11: General Post Office
12: Public Library
13: Grammar School
14: Council Offices
15: R.D.C. Offices
16: Cricket Ground
17: Football Ground
18: Gasholders
19: Dogs' Toilet
20: Waterfalls

A: Point of entry of route into the town
B: Point of departure

Above *Grey Friars Tower*
Right *Richmond Castle*

Richmond caters for all needs. On the riverside, toilets for dogs have been provided.

The Georgian Theatre, Richmond

Market Place, Richmond
Below *Castle Walk*

Below *A corner of Richmond*

The River Swale at Richmond

The Swale is one of the swiftest-flowing rivers in England and ranks amongst the loveliest, winding through a pleasant countryside and adding charm to the beauty of the surroundings. This is especially evident where it has carved a deep channel in the high moors of the upper valley between Keld, where it displays the excited exuberance of infancy, and Richmond; here it is wide and more sedate in middle age but is still hurried along its course by waterfalls and cascades and loses nothing in attractiveness by an urban environment. Soon after leaving Richmond, the river becomes more placid as it makes its way through the fertile farmlands of the Vale of York to join the Ure, the combined waters then becoming the River Ouse.

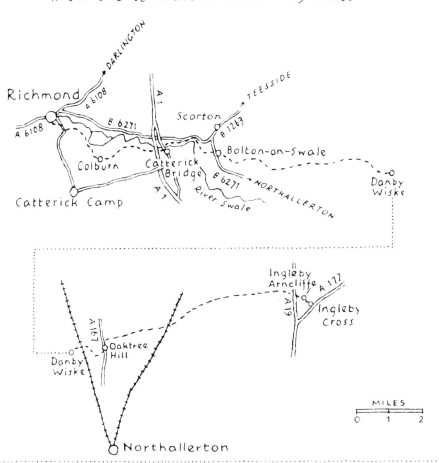

I CANNOT truthfully say that the crossing of the low country between the Yorkshire Dales and the Cleveland Hills was to my liking when planning the route of the Coast to Coast Walk. This area, locally known as the Vale of Mowbray, lies between two National Parks and is coveted by neither. Walkers who prefer to see hills in the landscape, or at least undulations, will vote this the least interesting part of the journey. It cannot be avoided. The high ground of the Dales ends abruptly near Richmond and a wide plain extends eastwards until terminated even more abruptly by the lofty Cleveland skyline, and the crossing from one to the other, in comparison with the journey thus far and thereafter, is tedious and lacks interest.

But don't get me wrong. The Vale of Mowbray is not an arid desert but an area of green fields, contented cows and scattered farmsteads in a quiet environment of undisturbed rustic serenity with scenes deserving of the brush of a painter of Constable's ability. Its one defect is that it has no hills, no viewpoints; visibility goes no further than the next hedgerow. Walkers who like to stride out at speed, ticking off the miles in rapid succession, and whose concern is to get from A to B in double-quick time will enjoy it. Visitors to this rural expanse are infrequent and people who walk with packs on their backs are regarded as eccentrics and find little available for their comfort. Farming comes first in the Vale of Mowbray.

Richmond formerly had a railway station, the terminus of a branch line from Darlington, and the route comes alongside it, following the Swale down-river and passing a sewage works that contrasts incongruously with the noble ruins of Easby Abbey seen on the opposite bank. Then a wood is entered on a path that hugs the river's edge, contributing mud to the boots, before turning up through the trees to a stile and a ruined farm, from which an indefinite track crosses fields to the village of Colburn.

Easby Abbey

Below *Woods near the River Swale*

Colburn   *Colburn Hall*

Colburn is an old village with a modern housing estate nearby, its most notable building being Colburn Hall, seen off-route on the left: this is an interesting rebuilt Tudor mansion with a separate Manor Hall.

From here a bridleway leads off to Catterick Bridge. At the time of my visit, the initial part was closed because of subsidence and a farmer graciously gave me permission to cross his land to rejoin it further along. This bridleway again brings the Swale into sight and continues pleasantly above its wooded banks, passing the site of St Giles Hospital in a loop of the river. A dull rumble ahead grows in volume as the walk proceeds, heralding the very busy and noisy A.1 with its unceasing streams of traffic and the Roman town of Cataractonium, now effectively effaced, alongside. Pedestrians are spared a hazardous crossing of the A.1 by an underpass from which a riverside path goes on to Catterick Bridge at a junction of roads, another animated scene when the Catterick Racecourse nearby is open for business.

The River Swale near St Giles

Catterick Bridge
Right *Beside the River Swale*

Refreshments are obtainable at Catterick Bridge but most walkers will prefer to get away from the traffic and noise here and seek the quiet of the riverside. This is quickly achieved by crossing the bridge and proceeding along a path on the north bank by the side of an ancient wall thought to be a Roman embankment. The path continues around a bend of the river until further progress is obstructed by a gravel works, the road alongside then being joined to a junction signposted Bolton-on-Swale, this village being the next objective.

St Mary's Church, Bolton-on-Swale

Right *The Jenkins Monument*

Bolton-on-Swale has a lovely church but the feature that attracts curious visitors is a monument in the graveyard dedicated to Henry Jenkins.

Believe it or not, Jenkins was born at nearby Ellerton in the year 1500 and died there in 1670 at the age of 169.

The monument was erected by public contributions in 1743 to commemorate his long life: a well-deserved recognition of an extraordinary achievement.

Field paths that do not accord with Ordnance Survey maps then lead alongside Bolton Beck to a quiet country road at Ellerton Hill.

At Ellerton Hill, there commences the longest continuous stretch of road walking on the entire journey – eight miles of it to Oaktree Hill. Tarmac roads are not favoured by most walkers whose preference is to travel on rough terrain, but here they are unavoidable. I tried to vary the route by resorting to footpaths indicated on the Ordnance maps only to be beaten back by barbed wire, wet ditches, too-friendly bovines and other obstacles: clearly this is not an area frequented by the walking fraternity. It is a waste of time to seek alternative ways and, with twenty-three miles on the day's itinerary, it is better to keep plodding along the roads in a monotonous left right left right left right . . .

Worse, the countryside is flat, with no heights to be seen until the later stages when the Cleveland Hills appear on the distant horizon but too remote to spur the feet; otherwise, there is nothing in sight but the immediate surroundings. This is a foreign land: it is strange to see fields fenced by hedges instead of the familiar stone walls, to have manure on the boots instead of honest mud. It is a landscape without contours: the ground in the first five miles lies wholly between 145 and 165 ft above the sea despite the 'moors' and 'hills' of the place-names. Those who believe the earth is flat will be mightily encouraged in their beliefs here. Marathon walkers who like to travel at speed on smooth and level surfaces will enjoy this section but most others will regard this as the dullest part of the journey, and think nostalgically of Lakeland and the Dales as they plod along.

But let's be fair to the Vale of Mowbray. Having said all that, I must also refer to the pleasant and tranquil environment, totally rural, the trees and twittering birds, the tidy husbandry, the mile after mile of verdant pastures. Here are Yorkshire's broad acres in person. Life may not be exciting and world events seem far away, but here is a quiet contentment that urban dwellers rarely experience.

In the absence of welcoming bed and breakfast and teas signs along the road, I looked forward with anticipatory eagerness to reaching the village of Danby Wiske: an intriguing name that promised much.

Streetlam

Danby Wiske

But Danby Wiske was a sore disappointment. It was an attractive little community but had not the charm I expected and all I could get to eat was a bag of crisps. At only 110 ft above sea level, Danby Wiske is the lowest point on the journey between the coastal extremities; to me it was a veritable Slough of Despond. However, I am assured by later walkers that the inn now offers refreshments galore and that a few cottages and farms on or near the route now cater for travellers on foot.

From Danby Wiske, the road-walking continues, the first of five important lines of communication that take advantage of the easy contours being soon reached: this is the main railway between King's Cross and Edinburgh. Then country lanes go forward to Oaktree Hill, a junction with the busy A.167 linking Northallerton and Darlington. This road carries a bus service that will take walkers who have had enough for the day into Northallerton, four miles south, where there is a choice of overnight accommodation. In this case, a return to Oaktree Hill can be made by the morning bus.

The railway

Oaktree Hill   Below *Site of the Battle of the Standards*

There is no cause to linger at Oaktree Hill unless waiting for a bus, and the noise and volume of traffic jars the nerves after the silence of the last few miles. The only place in the vicinity worthy of note is the site of the Battle of the Standards in fields half a mile south. Before the opening of Hampden Park and Wembley Stadium, the Scots and the English fought their battles wherever chance brought them together, this site being one such place and the date 22 October 1138 (1138–39 season). The English, playing at home, won this match.

The lane from Oaktree Hill

Below *Moor House*

Escape from the busy A.167 is provided by a gated grassy lane leading off the road north of Oaktree Hill, a sylvan avenue by comparison. Along here at last a contour is crossed and a height of 200 feet attained without undue effort, leaving one to wonder afresh why so many place-names in this low-lying countryside incorporate the words 'hill' and 'moor' when there are none to be seen and only the slightest of undulations to justify them. The lane debouches onto a minor road, Deighton Lane, and here my troubles as a route planner reached a crescendo.

My Ordnance Survey map promised me a direct route ahead from Deighton Lane by a linking of footpaths through fields over a distance of almost three miles to Low Moor Lane. Initially, there was no difficulty in reaching the farm of Moor House along its access road but there was no sign of a continuation beyond and the occupants looked blank when asked where the footpath was but gave me permission to cross their fields in the direction indicated by the map. Then followed a most frustrating exercise trying to trace invisible paths, negotiating blocked stiles and barbed wire fences, floundering across wet dykes and thrusting through thorn hedges with a strong suspicion of trespass although the map said O.K.

At one point, I startled a farmer by suddenly appearing from a hedge: he was a friendly fellow and told me he had no knowledge of a right of way and, although he had lived here for donkey's years, he had never before seen anyone walking through his fields. Difficulties persisted, a bull adding to my discomfort, until farm roads gave an easier passage to another minor road, from which a farm access road led to a level crossing of the Northallerton to Teesside railway.

On returning home, I wrote to the Clerk of the County Council, telling him of my experiences on the rights of way in his district, especially on this section, and requesting that he ask the County Surveyor to travel the route and clear out the obstructions in anticipation of the guidebook I was writing for early publication. This task the Surveyor must have carried out expeditiously and efficiently. I expected howls of protest from the farmers but although thousands of walkers have followed in my steps, not one has ever complained of any impediments to progress here.

I understand that the Ramblers' Association have contributed to the easier passage of walkers by waymarking the route in places where doubts may arise. Thanks, R.A.

Harlsey Grove: a moated farmstead

Rights of Way

A right of way is defined as "a right established by usage to pass over another's land."

Public roads are dedicated for the use of the public at large, on wheels or on foot, and are therefore rights of way unless prohibition is imposed on specified forms of progression (pedestrians on motorways, for example) by the highways authorities.

Private roads, including most farm access roads, have no rights of way unless such are established by use and recorded on the footpath maps maintained by the local authorities for the district.

Common ground may be freely wandered over by all.

What are more usually referred to as walkers' rights of way are *public footpaths* and *bridleways* over private land. Such rights may be legally provided in title deeds or they may simply have developed by the tread of feet over a period so long that "the memory of man runneth not to the contrary." Where rights of way do exist it is incumbent upon the owner or tenant to permit through access by means of stiles or gates and keep the route free from hazard. Where a public footpath is in general use these conditions are invariably observed, but where little or no use is made of rights of way by the public there is a natural tendency to disregard their existence and cease to maintain them. This happens frequently in the section from Richmond to Ingleby Cross, where the footpaths are not only invisible on the ground but often blocked by obstructions, including bulls.

The rights of way incorporated in this section of the route are not free from hazards at the time of writing, but the difficulties in negotiating them experienced by the author have been reported in gruesome detail to the North Riding County Council, who have kindly undertaken a survey, as the result of which a smoother passage can be expected by future travellers.

Reproduced above is a page from the guidebook relating to rights of way in this area.

Sheep near Sydal Lodge   Below *The field down to the footbridge*

Avoiding oncoming trains and safely negotiating the level crossing, the route presents fewer complications. A footpath goes forward to enter Low Moor Lane, this leading unerringly to a meeting of more minor roads. Across a T-junction is the imposing gateway of a farm road-cum-drive to Sydal Lodge, and beyond the buildings a pathless field goes down to a footbridge over a little stream in a pretty dell where cows love to congregate for a gossip.

Above *The footbridge over the river*
Right *Brecken Hill*

The stream is the sluggish River Wiske, last seen at Danby and destined to meander aimlessly and hopefully in search of contours that would give it an objective to aim for. From the footbridge, there is a slight ascent to the derelict buildings of Brecken Hill, where an improving cart-track winds along past other farms and descends slightly to reach the very busy double carriageway of the A.19 linking Northallerton and Stockton-on-Tees.

Crossing the A.19, which speeding vehicles regard as a race-track, is a hazardous ordeal for tired limbs; if safely accomplished the calmer environment of a by-road leading into the village of Ingleby Arncliffe (ice-cream at the post office) can be enjoyed in the knowledge that the last lap of a long day's march is now under foot. The Cleveland Hills loom large ahead, promising more exciting walking tomorrow, so flagging spirits rise on the short descent by road to Ingleby Cross.

Left *Ingleby Arncliffe*

Below *The Cleveland Hills from Ingleby Arncliffe*

Ingleby Cross

Ingleby Cross, journey's end for the day, is situated on another busy road, the A.172 to Middlesbrough. There is not much of it, but set back from the junction near the cross is the Blue Bell Inn with recently improved accommodation for walkers, and, for wise virgins who have booked in advance, this is the place to take off the boots and enjoy a deserved evening's relaxation. Others, less wise and less fortunate, will find a large hotel, the Cleveland Tontine, a short distance south along the road. Youth hostellers will find the foot of their rainbow a mile further along tomorrow's route.

At Ingleby Cross there is cause for immense satisfaction. The North York Moors National Park is entered here and there lies ahead four splendid days to be spent on a high-level traverse of heather-clad moors, fifty miles of lovely scenery and wide panoramas on a well-defined path across an unspoilt wilderness, and, at the end of it, the North Sea and fulfilment of a cherished ambition. A mouth-watering prospect!

THE NORTH YORK MOORS

The broad expanse of moorland extending for thirty miles from the Vale of Mowbray to the east coast, heatherclad, unenclosed, uninhabited, remote from industry and noise and free of traffic, is a magnificent territory for the walker: open country like the Pennines but more handsome and colourful – and friendlier by far. It is a wilderness crossed by few roads but many ancient tracks, a plateau high above the valleys, yet of sleek and rounded slopes and easy gradients where one can wander at will and enjoy complete freedom; an elevated desert neither arid nor sterile but abounding in interest and beauty.

And not only the walker will find delight here. For the archaeologist, the researcher into past history, the moors tell the story of the primitive people who settled here ages ago when climatic conditions were kinder for a time and the hills, then wooded, served both as home and hunting ground: their cairns and earthworks, barrows and burial mounds remain to this day remarkably profuse; of the Romans who flitted briefly across the scene leaving little of present interest excepting a road, recently partially restored, and signal stations; of Scandinavian invaders later, who first set the patterns of community life that have survived. Most of the village names are of Norse or Danish origin.

The botanist and naturalist, the geologist and mineralogist, are all catered for on the wild hills and in the sheltered valleys; the artist and photographer will enthuse over the variations of landscape. Today it is hard to believe that these uplands were formerly exploited for the wealth below the surface, but in fact they have been worked extensively for iron and coal and for the rarer jet and alum. These industries are now all abandoned and nature is hiding their traces although the tracks of the mineral railways, the iron workings and jet spoil-heaps are likely to be permanent reminders. New industries of recent date are producing natural gas and potash while forestry operations are spreading along the hillsides; quite incongruous in an area remarkable for its prehistoric relics is an ultra-modern Ballistic Missile Early Warning Station.

The geographical boundaries of the area are clearly defined by surrounding valleys. To the north is Teesside, to the west the Vale of Mowbray, to the south the Vale of Pickering, and the eastern boundary is the coastal strip: all low-lying land, and in their midst rises sharply the high plateau with its backbone on a west—east axis and of consistent altitude but indented by deep valleys, longer in the south where the slopes are gentler than they are northwards. Separating the valleys are lofty ridges. Each valley has its stream feeding one of three main rivers: the Esk (north), the Rye and the Derwent (south).

The absence of walls and fences gives a rare feeling of freedom to expeditions along the crest, and two pedestrian routes recently inaugurated are proving very popular. One is Lyke Wake Walk, an arduous forty-miler having a time limit of twenty-four hours, the other is the 100-mile marathon known as the Cleveland Way. With both, as instigator of one and supporter of the other, the name of Bill Cowley is indelibly associated. The Coast to Coast walk makes acquaintance with each one.

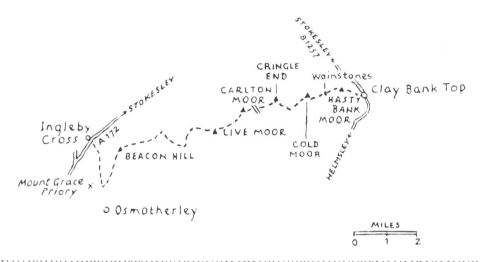

A STRONG walker could do this section and the next together in the course of a day's march but have little time for contemplation of the scenery. It is preferable, however, to travel leisurely over the next stage to the road at Clay Bank Top – a splendid walk visiting six fell tops. The one and only disadvantage is that a detour must be made off-route along the road to find a night's lodging unless sleeping equipment is being carried. The North York Moors is the one place above all others where a tent-dweller scores heavily.

With a packed lunch in the rucksack, the lane alongside the inn at Ingleby Cross is followed to the hamlet of Arncliffe where there is a church and a hall, the latter a handsome Georgian house designed by John Carr of York in 1754. The high ground of the moors rises immediately behind, the steep slope cloaked by Arncliffe Wood, but is better gained by first using a forest road due south until abreast of Mount Grace Priory, which should certainly be visited although off-route (path from Park House).

Arncliffe Church

Mount Grace Priory

Dating from 1398, Mount Grace Priory is one of the finest surviving examples of the few Carthusian foundations in this country. The monks lived here in seclusion, almost as hermits, each isolated in his own cell with a garden, observing a rule of strict silence. The arrangement of the monks' quarters around a large walled cloister can be clearly seen. The central building within the grounds of the Priory was the church, the tower being still intact. Adjoining is the former Priory guest house, still partly in use. The ruins are open to the public on payment of an admission charge, and maintained by English Heritage.

The forest road is rejoined after the detour to Mount Grace Priory and soon reaches the forest boundary. At this point the village of Osmotherley is only a few minutes away and can be visited if supplies are needed. At the forest boundary, the route turns left on a signposted path, rising steadily through trees and reaching a TV booster station of revolting appearance, its many contraptions being like apparitions from outer space. Then, just beyond, the open moorland of Beacon Hill is reached, the summit marked by an Ordnance column that is also a symbol of optimism: here starts the gruelling Lyke Wake Walk, this route being way-marked by black discs.

Beacon Hill is the first of the day's six summits. Although only 982 ft above sea level, it is a superb

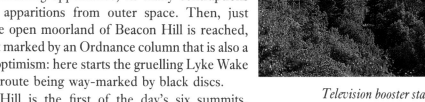

Television booster station on Beacon Hill

viewpoint, the panorama being greatly enhanced by the abrupt rise from the plains. Southwards, apparently stretching to the ends of the earth, is the Vale of York; westwards is the long line of Pennines beyond the flat lands of yesterday, a conspicuous indentation indicating Swaledale; northwards the hills of Durham are seen across the valley of the Tees. Most attention, however, will be focused on the prospect eastwards, where a range of beckoning hills indicates the next area of the walk.

Looking east from Beacon Hill

A gate on Beacon Hill at the time of my visit bore the following notice:

Be ye man or be ye woman
Be ye going or be ye comin
Be ye soon or be ye late
Be ye sure to shut this gate.

Ripon C. S. School,
21st June 1968.

Having obeyed this injunction, walkers can prepare for one of the best days ever; a sequence of ups and downs on an invigorating switchback over a succession of lovely hills blessed with gentle gradients. Beacon Hill is left along a clear path heading for the promised land; here and for several miles onwards, the route is the same as the Lyke Wake Walk and is doubly trodden. A motor road that has evolved from an ancient drove road is crossed at Scarth Nick, a ravine caused by a geological fault between Scarth Wood Moor, which has Bronze Age remains, and Near Moor ahead. A car park at Scarth Nick is much patronised by motorists wishing to exercise their atrophied legs. Across the road, there is a gentle descent into the pastoral valley of Scugdale.

The approach to Scarsdale

Scugdale is cultivated and inhabited. There are scattered houses and farms and a small complex of buildings at Huthwaite Green, all linked by a valley road to the village of Swainby. A stream, Scugdale Beck, threads the valley, flowing north from the moors to join the River Leven, and the route follows a pleasant lane upstream until a bridge affords a crossing to the road and Huthwaite Green in an area of old iron mine workings. Above the hamlet, a path climbs to the broad top of Live Moor, 1025 ft, where a cairn built on a tumulus commands a view of the next height forward on the ridge, Carlton Moor.

A lane in Scugdale

The cairn on Live Moor, looking to Carlton Moor

From Live Moor, the path continues along the ridge which here is a watershed between the gathering grounds of the Ouse and the Tees. The northern edge forms a small escarpment, at the base of which can be seen the pink and white spoil heaps of old jet mines, these industrial relics appearing in a long line but maintaining the same contour.

The path rises in a sweeping curve up the slopes of Carlton Moor where, when the gradient eases, a surprise awaits. At the time of my visit, the landscape here was eerily lunar: for half a mile the heather had been newly stripped off and the surface bulldozed and levelled to make runways for the Newcastle and Teesside Gliding Club, the hangars and clubhouse being nearby. This arid man-made desert has now been grassed over.

So Carlton Moor, formerly a place of work, has become a place of leisure. Gliding is a fine sport, a thrilling and graceful exercise, creating neither noise nor litter, but not even the most ardent enthusiast will claim that the landscape has been improved by its conversion to runways, and some may even concede that a large tract of natural beauty has been despoiled. It is perhaps unfair for an 'off-comer' to comment adversely on happenings here, but I must say that if such an operation had been planned for the top of Helvellyn all hell would have been let loose.

The summit of Carlton Moor, 1338 ft, is reached along the rim of the escarpment and marked by a boundary stone and an Ordnance column. This is another splendid viewpoint, an airy perch with an uninterrupted prospect of Teesside. Conspicuous in the mid-distance is the sharp peak of Roseberry Topping, hacked by quarrying operations into a miniature Matterhorn; the monument to Captain Cook on Easby Moor, a little nearer, can also be seen. Below the sharp fall of the summit are more abandoned jet workings. Eastwards, across a depression, is the next height on the ridge, Cringle Moor.

The summit of Carlton Moor looking to Cringle Moor

Old Alum Mine, Carlton Bank

Below *Summit 'furnishings', Crinkle End*

A rough descent follows, passing along the edge of a disused alum mine that has left a crater and radically altered the natural contours of the ground, to the deep depression of Carlton Bank Top, crossed by a minor road. Ahead is a choice of tracks leading up to the stony promontory of Cringle End, a much-visited viewpoint furnished with a boundary post, a stone seat and a view indicator, the latter a memorial to Alec Falconer (1884–1968) who, under the pseudonym of 'Rambler', was a champion of walkers' interests.

A short stroll through heather leads to the summit of Cringle Moor, at 1427 ft the greatest elevation so far reached on the range and the second highest on the Cleveland Hills and further distinguished by a steep and craggy declivity from its northern rim. The summit cairn is superimposed on a tumulus. Seen ahead now across a wide saddle is the next height to be climbed, Cold Moor.

Cold Moor from Cringle Moor   Below *Summit cairn, Cringle Moor*

After descending from Cringle Moor, the walled enclosures on the saddle are crossed on a clear path that then ascends to the airy dome of Cold Moor, 1317 ft, a pleasant summit of heather and bilberry with a view forward to the last height of the day, Hasty Bank, identified by an outcrop of rocks, the Wainstones, on the near side of its broad top.

Cringle Moor from Cold Moor

Below *Hasty Bank from Cold Moor*

The Wainstones:
the lower rocks

The Wainstones:
the upper rocks

Naked rock is not a feature of the North York Moors, which are more notable for rich surface vegetation. It occurs mainly and infrequently in the low cliffs of the escarpments, but at the Wainstones appears as a grotesque collection of fanged pinnacles, some of which provide short rock climbs while others offer shelter from the elements. Everybody stops here, to rest, to eat, to explore or to take photographs: it is an obvious place for a halt. This is the only obstacle in the entire range where progress is impeded by a natural formation, but there are no difficulties of negotiation, a steep but simple path having been worn between the rocks to arrive on easy ground above and the flat top of Hasty Bank.

Urra Moor from Hasty Bank

Overleaf *Towards Teeside from the Wainstones*

The traverse of Hasty Bank, 1304 ft, is a gentle promenade with no problems and a fine panorama; there is an uninterrupted view forward to the next section of the walk, over Urra Moor, but separated from it by a deep trench carrying the B.1257 road linking Helmsley and Stokesley. A rough descent brings the tarmac underfoot at the highest point of the road, Hagg Gate, better known as Clay Bank Top.

Clay Bank Top is an oasis of trees and, in the spring, bluebells, welcome after the austerity of the moors. This is the place to decide what to do next: the light is fading and shelter for the night must be sought except by those who carry their beds on their backs. The road has an infrequent bus service, Helmsley to Middlesbrough, and it is too much to hope that arrival here will coincide with a passing bus. There is, however, a large car park, and although still in a state of exultant delight at the successful completion of a splendid day's walk, it may be possible, by feigning distress, to persuade a sympathetic motorist to offer a lift down the road to the village of Great Broughton (2½ miles) or better still if supplies are needed for the next two shop-less days, to the market town of Stokesley (5 miles). Hitch-hiking is permissible off-route! If this is done, of course a return to Clay Bank Top next morning, on foot or on wheels, is necessary to resume the journey.

Above *Clay Bank Top*
Opposite *Looking back from Cold Moor to the Wainstones*

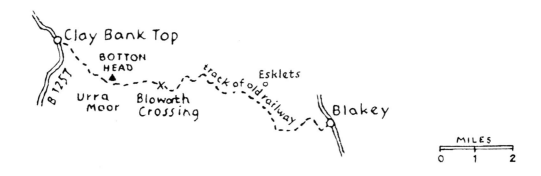

CLAY BANK TOP to BLAKEY : 9¼ miles

THERE is a steady rise from Clay Bank Top to the broad upland expanse of Urra Moor and the highest ground of the North York Moors, but thereafter the walking is very easy, especially when the track of the old Rosedale railway is joined, this providing the fastest travelling of the whole journey. There are no habitations until the inn at Blakey is reached and if no accommodation is available here, it may be necessary to continue on the next section into Eskdale, making the day's march eighteen miles but not beyond the ability of an average walker. It is advisable, therefore, to arrive at Blakey in the early afternoon. The route to Blakey is wholly on the line of the Lyke Wake Walk, simple to follow, and interesting and enjoyable throughout, and has lovely views down into the valleys draining from the moors.

The Forestry Commission owns much of the land around Clay Bank and Urra Moor and there are plantations both mature and immature but they do not impede progress. The route crosses the B.1257 and after an initial curve heads in a straight line on an old packhorse road with boundary stones alongside. It rises along Carr Ridge to the broad top of Urra Moor, passing on the way, down the hillside on the right, some ancient earthworks known locally as Cromwell's Trenches. As height is gained and the slope eases, there is a fine retrospective view of the hills crossed in yesterday's trek.

The moon rises over Urra Moor

Cringle Moor, Cold Moor and Hasty Bank from Urra Moor

Urra Moor is an area abounding in historic interest. In addition to the packhorse road, now adapted as a fire break and which in places displays its original paving and has inscribed boundary stones, there are the tumuli and barrows of an early civilisation. The highest part of the moor, Botton Head, has the distinction of having the greatest elevation on the North York Moors, the actual summit, 1491 ft, being a round barrow or burial ground with the appropriate name of Round Hill: it is indicated by an Ordnance column to the left of the road.

Round Hill, Botton Head

On the roadside opposite Round Hill is the Hand Stone, a guidepost inscribed with lettering and pointing hands, and as the walk proceeds the Face Stone is met, this having a carved face, and further along, the Red Stone; these are thought to have been erected in the early years of the eighteenth century although possibly older.

The Hand Stone *The Face Stone* *The Red Stone*

The road descends slightly, the paving here being visible. Railway enthusiasts in particular should note the straight rising line of the incline that once carried the Rosedale mineral railway from the valley up to moor level. The track of this railway is joined near Bloworth Crossing, still with a gate, where the line crossed an old moorland road.

The railway incline
Right *Bloworth Crossing*

At Bloworth Crossing, the walking becomes dead easy as the railway track is followed for six miles around many sinuous curves and on the same contour all the way. The rails have been taken up and the permanent way has grown grass, but it offers a journey of pure delight to walkers with youthful minds who can imagine themselves speeding along in charge of a locomotive.

THE ROSEDALE IRONSTONE RAILWAY

The Rosedale Branch was constructed in 1861, when the North Eastern Railway extended its lines in Cleveland by incorporating a mineral line, replacing it by a single standard-gauge track and continuing it by means of a mile-long incline across the high moors at an elevation of around 1300' for ten miles to the ironstone mines in Rosedale — a considerable engineering achievement, the contours being so closely followed that, throughout a long passage across several watersheds, cuttings, embankments and levelling sufficed to carry the line around the heads of intervening valleys without the use of any bridges or tunnels. The track was unenclosed by fences and had no signalling equipment, operation being controlled by staff based on Blakey Ridge. This remarkable enterprise was undertaken to convey the high-grade iron ore mined on the Rosedale hillsides, which had in fact been worked from a very early date, possibly for two thousand years, as evidenced by ancient furnaces, and was enjoying a booming prosperity in the middle of last century. Road transport via Pickering was inadequate to cope with the output; the construction of a high-level railway over the moors, linking with other lines that served the big blast furnaces of Teesside and Durham, was a bold venture, and, despite storms and blizzards, appears to have well succeeded, upwards of ten million tons of iron ore being conveyed along it. Only freight trains used the line but occasionally a few passengers were carried.

The railway as originally laid entered Rosedale by way of Blakey Ridge and terminated at the Bank Top mines on the west side of the valley, where the main workings were located and which today can be identified by a prominent chimney,* one of the many relics still to be seen. In 1865 it was extended by a branch running around the head of the valley to mines on the eastern flank from the staff control point at Blakey, which then became a junction.

By the turn of the century ironstone production was in decline and the railway less in demand, and finally it was closed and dismantled in 1929. The line was lonely and isolated, and threatened by extreme weather conditions, but the regular passage of freight trains brought a pulse of life to the wilderness through which they passed. Today the track is still there, but it is silent; yet even in death it has lost nothing of its grace and dignity but remains a mute and inspiring monument to the men who planned and built it over a century ago, a permanent way that will remain permanent, a reminder of an achievement that deserves to be, and will be, long remembered.

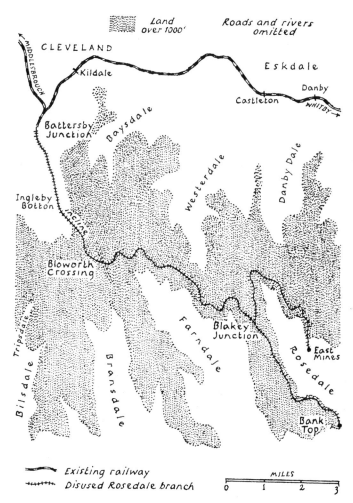

A fascinating description of the Rosedale mines and railway is found in a booklet, *A History of Rosedale* by Raymond H. Hayes, published by The North York Moors National Park, 1985, price £2.50.

Chimney demolished 1972

Sinuous curves of the old railway

The railway track runs below the crest of the ridge on the south side and affords beautiful views down and along the valleys descending to the Vale of Pickering. Most prominently seen are Bransdale, Farndale and Rosedale. Farndale, in particular, remains in view for a few miles as the track skirts the head of this valley.

Farndale   Opposite *Biskey Howe*

Looking down into the lovely reaches of Farndale, renowned for its springtime display of daffodils, it seems unbelievable that its tranquillity was threatened a few years ago by men with souls so dead, with visions so clouded, with appreciation of natural beauty so withered, that they actually schemed to flood the valley with water permanently by constructing a large reservoir. Happily, the common sense of others prevailed. Farndale is still undisturbed, still a sylvan Arcadia.

Youth hostellers will probably leave the railway track at the end of a long embankment where a notice board indicates a path that leads to the derelict farm of Esklets and goes forward into Westerdale for a night at the hostel in that valley. This path, as far as Esklets, is also used by Lyke Wake walkers as a recommended alternative, but the Coast to Coast route continues along the railway track, now seeming endless. In course of time, however, the chimneys of a habitation are seen and, now tired of playing at being trains, walkers can make a beeline to it, leaving the track to go forward to the site of Blakey Junction. The building is the Lion Inn.

The Lion Inn at Blakey

Dating from 1553, the Lion is a bleak and isolated inn set back from a moorland road that crosses the tops into Eskdale. Situated amongst decayed relics of industry, its patrons are no longer ironworkers and coalminers; today it is a port of call for travellers in cars or on foot. It stands high above Rosedale, another very lovely valley despite the pockmarking of abandoned mines on the enclosing hillsides. When I was last here, no accommodation was available for visitors but I understand that it is now provided.

Behind the inn, and only two minutes away, is Biskey Howe, a tumulus excavated to make a sheltered and secluded hollow for cockfighting; it is, for this reason, alternatively known as Cockpit Hill.

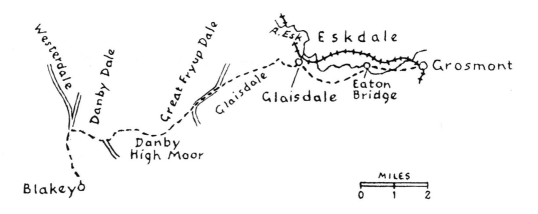

THE penultimate day. The watershed is crossed, the wild moors left behind and a descent made into the beautiful valley of Eskdale. The loneliness of the last few days is ended by a mingling with fellow creatures and the companionship of a lovely river, and the silences of the heights replaced by the sounds of civilisation; there are houses and shops again and even an *active* railway. The landscape, no longer sombre, becomes richly wooded and verdant, and the day's walk is designed to ensure that there is time to enjoy it at a leisurely pace.

The Lyke Wake Walk departs from the Lion Inn at Blakey by resuming the old railway track on a circuit of the head of Rosedale amongst the untidy workings of abandoned pits and mines, but the Coast to Coast Walk heads north along the road, taking advantage of ample grass verges, to inspect relics of earlier age. The first of these is a boundary stone on the roadside with the odd name, for a stone, of Margery Bradley, or Old Margery as it is sometimes called although there is no young one around. At this point, the other branch of the Lyke Wake Walk crosses the road to head east, and its familiar black disc waymarkings will not be seen again. Further along there is a modern roadside memorial to Frank Elgee, and just beyond the first of two ancient monuments, the Ralph Crosses. This is young Ralph, with a hollowed top to contain coins donated for needy travellers. Old Ralph is seen a short distance away across the moor. Here there is a junction of unenclosed roads, the one heading east now being followed and soon coming alongside the White Cross, a squat stone better known as Fat Betty.

Frank Elgee Memorial

Old Margery
Old Ralph

Young Ralph
Fat Betty

The exposed area around the Ralph Crosses, at a height around 1400 ft, is an obvious main watershed, all the northern slopes draining into Eskdale. Southwards there is a fine view of the full length of Rosedale stretching for many miles to the plains beyond and, after centuries of industrial activity, once again a tranquil rural sanctuary of great charm.

Rosedale

Just beyond Fat Betty, walking on the tarmac can be avoided by following a line of white boundary stones across the moor to reach a gravelly cart-track heading north over the watershed and bound for Fryup, this soon revealing a far-reaching prospect of the wooded valley of Eskdale but still some miles ahead. The geographical formation of the northern slopes is unusual: instead of the expected gradual decline from the watershed, here named Danby High Moor (and, incidentally, having several Bronze Age sites), the ground is furrowed into a series of distinct descending ridges separated by deep valleys and appearing in plan like the spokes of a wheel. It is important to identify the route of descent correctly: this lies along Glaisdale Rigg, the ridge between Great Fryup Dale and Glaisdale.

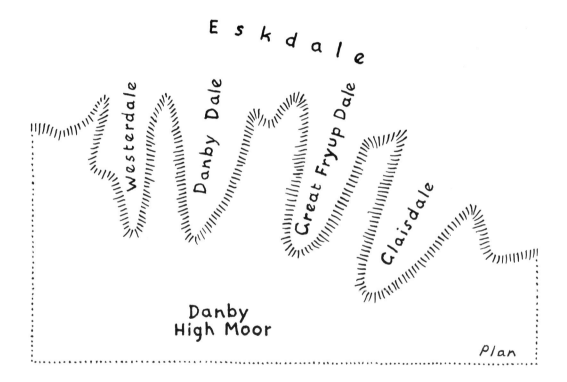

After half a mile along the Fryup cart-track, it is forsaken in favour of a branch to the right leading to a solitary building now in sight. This is Trough House, a shooting–box roughly furnished and affording such excellent shelter that one almost wishes for rain to take advantage of it. Beyond, the path deteriorates in an area of old coal pits and is overgrown with heather, bracken and rushes although its course is plain to see as it rounds the head of Great Fryup Dale, of which there is a full-length view, and slants down now heading directly for Glaisdale. Here it joins an unenclosed motor road, this being followed until, beyond a large well-built cairn, a path turns off the road and gives access to Glaisdale Rigg, pursuing a direct course along the crest of this ridge.

Glaisdale Rigg is a joy to tread. It leads un-erringly down to the valley on a distinct path that was once a highway, as the many standing stones testify: one is inscribed 'Whitby Road'. Walking along this elevated crest is easy, the pace being accelerated as steps are impelled by the early prospect of ice cream and lemonade and other innocent delights of the flesh, with the views forward of Eskdale increasing in beauty as the valley is seen more intimately.

At the foot of the ridge a road is joined and the attractive village of Glaisdale entered in a search for a place to spend some money.

The wilderness days are over.

Cairn on Glaisdale Rigg
Below *Eskdale from Glaisdale Ridge*

Glaisdale village

Below *The station at Glaisdale*

At Glaisdale, a first acquaintance with the River Esk can and should be made, and the place to do this is at the early seventeenth-century Beggar's Bridge, which spans the river in a single graceful arch amidst lovely scenery.

At Beggar's Bridge, a first acquaintance is also made with the Eskdale railway which, interweaving with the river, threads a sylvan course through the valley on a journey of scenic delight. Glaisdale station is nearby.

From the railway bridge a path, initially steep, enters East Arncliffe Wood and continues downriver, overgrown in places but defined by rough paving with stone slabs; this is a natural woodland providing a canopy of foliage and a welcome change from the bleakness of the moors. The path emerges from the trees and joins a road that goes forward to Egton Bridge.

East Arncliffe Wood

The River Esk at Egton Bridge

The surroundings of Egton Bridge are beautiful. Here is the Esk again, bordered by a wealth of noble trees and verdant pastures, with extensive woodlands draping the hillsides and descending to the valley. The scenery is of a high order but with one jarring feature: the iron river bridge offends the eye and is totally out of character; the crossing deserves stone arches. There are buildings of distinction here. Egton Manor set in spacious grounds, is now an estate office, and nearby the Roman Catholic Church has distinctive features worth inspection, notably the coloured bas relief panels on the exterior walls and the ornate decorations internally on the ribbed roof.

At Egton Bridge, in its sequestered and peaceful setting, there is little awareness of the desolate and inhospitable moors around which, however, reveal much of archaeological interest with traces both of prehistoric origin and of the Roman occupation of the area.

The village of Egton is a mile north of the river and off-route. It was once famous for its markets and fairs and now has an annual gooseberry show to add to the unique attractions of the district. This part of Eskdale appeals greatly to visitors as the too many caravan sites testify. One cannot blame town-dwellers for seeking relaxation from worldly pressures in the countryside and indeed can applaud them for doing so, but crowded caravan communities, which never enhance a landscape and too often spoil it, are surely not the ideal means of escape. Still, every man to his own tastes. I am considered eccentric for preferring the lonely hilltops.

Egton Manor

Below *The Roman Catholic Church, Egton Bridge*

The walk continues on a pleasant lane along the north boundary of Egton Manor. This is an estate road, now barred to vehicles: that this was not always so is shown by a notice affixed to a building midway that still displays details of tolls charged to former users. The list is comprehensive and caters not only for the living but the dead (hearse 6d). The railway crosses from Egton station and the Esk comes alongside as the lane enters a road that crosses the river and leads into the village of Grosmont.

At Grosmont (pronounced Gro-mont) the traveller down the valley of the Esk first becomes aware, albeit slightly, of urban influences. There are still the steep declivities to the river, the rich woodlands that so characterise the higher reaches, but the railway junction, the debris of abandoned iron works and blast furnaces, and a faint air of commercialism suggest that the best of the scenery has been left behind. Nevertheless, Grosmont is an excellent centre for touring the district by both road and rail; there are shops, and accommodation is on offer. A priory of the Prandimontine order existed here from around 1200 onwards, but the present needs of the Anglican community are now served by a church set back from the houses in a hanging garden of trees by the river. Road access to the village is very steep on both sides, which would appear to explain the absence of a bus service.

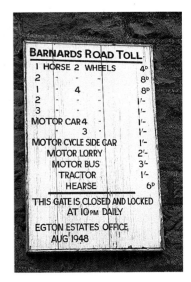

Toll board on the estate road

Below *Bridge over the Esk at Grosmont*

For railway enthusiasts, the great attraction of Grosmont is the railway station. Here they will suffer convulsions of unbridled joy at the sight of steam locomotives, defying modern techniques of construction, still working hard and still giving an almost-forgotten pleasure to their passengers.

The railway from Whitby to Pickering, leaving the Eskdale line at Grosmont, followed a tortuous course through scenery of rare beauty, and popular opinion considered it to be one of the finest and most spectacular railways in the country. It was a creation of George Stephenson. But the time came when the railway authorities considered its day was done and closed it like so many others, and a notable engineering achievement was destined to become yet another historical relic.

The line came to life again, however, when a band of enthusiasts, the North York Moors Railway Society, succeeded in their valiant efforts to preserve and continue the line privately on the section from Grosmont to Goathland, since when it has been further extended, using steam locomotives and rolling stock they have acquired. They have done well. George Stephenson would have approved.

Preserved engine at Grosmont

Grosmont

Below *Grosmont Church*

Grosmont is the end of the day's walk and provides overnight lodgings for travellers. With only one day's march ahead, and 175 miles already trampled underfoot, Coast to Coast walkers may feel they have earned a mild anticipatory celebration. Why not? Tomorrow, all being well, will see the end of the journey.

They may wish for a more varied evening's jollification than Grosmont can offer and, if so, the answer is at hand. Whitby is only a few miles away on the railway, and those who have never seen this picturesque fishing port should certainly take this opportunity to do so, visiting the Abbey and the harbour and paying homage to Captain Cook, the town's greatest export, before touring the public bars. The morning train will return them to Grosmont.

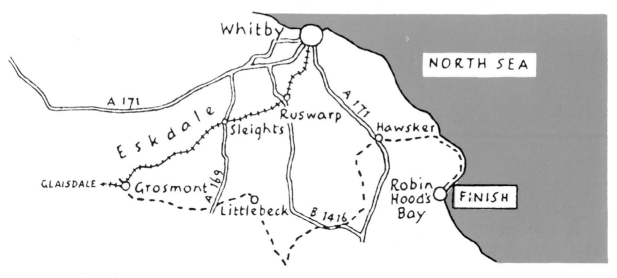

POSITIVELY the last lap. This final day's walk is notable for its variety and contrasts of scenery. Eskdale is left behind and there is a further visit to heather moors, this time rewarded by a first glimpse of the North Sea. A descent follows to a most delightful rural retreat and the highest waterfall yet seen on the journey, and then, in conclusion, a traverse along the tops of sea cliffs and, at the end, Robin Hood's Bay.

Departure from Grosmont is made along the road rising steeply east from the village to reach the open expanse of Sleights Moor, where a visit may be made out of curiosity to see two features indicated on Ordnance maps, Low Bride Stones and High Bride Stones, by a slight deviation. The former is a disappointment, being merely a few boulders almost hidden by rushes in a swamp; more impressive is the group of High Bride Stones, some standing and some fallen. Opposite the latter, the road is crossed and a beeline due east is made to a prominent tumulus, Flat Howe.

Low Bride Stones　　　　　　　　　　　　　　　　　　*High Bride Stones*

Flat Howe

Arrival at the Flat Howe tumulus is a thrilling moment. Here for the first time on the journey is a sight that has been eagerly anticipated: the Promised Sea. There is not a shadow of doubt. Ahead, some miles distant, is a level horizon of water. It is the North Sea at last.

Apart from this exciting prospect, there is an extensive all-round view. Whitby and its Abbey are seen etched against the sea; then to the right is the hinterland of the coastal cliffs, a break in the land outline indicating the position of Robin Hood's Bay; south are the mammoth 'golf balls' of the Fylingdales Early Warning Station, a modern apparition that seems ludicrous especially when the larks are singing. The 3000-year-old corpses beneath this burial ground must surely be turning in their graves.

Fylingdales   Below *Littlebeck*

The beeline is continued through pathless heather to the busy Whitby—Pickering highway, reaching it where a signpost points the way, but not for motors, to Littlebeck. Then follows a descent to this tiny hamlet, set in a secluded and sheltered valley amid scenery of bewitching beauty; a heaven on earth in exquisite miniature. Here a path is taken amongst trees, with a sparkling stream as companion, to the higher reaches of the valley.

The path rises gently to a massive boulder, out of which, amazingly, has been carved a large shelter with seats; in beautiful lettering the name The Hermitage, the year 1790 and the initials G. C. are inscribed on the boulder. Here the Falling Foss Nature Trail is joined and the route coincides with it for the next mile, passing the grounds of Newton House Field Centre and then coming alongside a graceful waterfall in a setting of great charm, a highlight of the walk. This is Falling Foss, a single plunge of 67 ft.

The Hermitage
Below *The footbridge to Falling Foss*

Opposite *Falling Foss*

The popularity of Falling Foss and the nature trail becomes evident on proceeding further upstream, a Trailside Museum being passed and, on emerging from the trees, a car park for visitors, where descriptive leaflets are obtainable, and a public access road. These facilities are a fairly recent innovation and come as a big surprise to anyone using out-of-date maps. The route goes along the access road as far as a farm, where it is left to cross the heather of Sneaton Low Moor, which is swampy in places, but who cares about wet feet when Robin Hood's Bay is so near? A T-junction of motor roads is reached, one going straight ahead to Hawsker, the next objective, and preferable in bad weather. The planned route, however, turns right along the B.1416, which is surprisingly busy for a country road, the reason being that it is used by traffic between Scarborough and Teesside to bypass Whitby, but peace and quiet are soon restored to the walk by a crossing of Graystones Hill, again in heather, passing a solitary ancient monument, Portgate Cross. Streams of traffic now appear on the Whitby—Scarborough road, the A.171, which can be entered at a gate where a signpost gives the thrilling news that a branch road leads to Robin Hood's Bay, only two miles distant. From this point, journey's end can be reached in half an hour, but this would be cheating and in any case is a noisy and crowded approach to the bay. The Coast to Coast route prefers a quiet and pleasant roundabout way to finish the walk, as it started, by a traverse along coastal cliffs, and heads due north over the moor to join a lane that debouches on a country road leading to the village of Hawsker.

Portgate Cross on Graystones Hill

Hawsker (in two parts, High and Low) is an upland village, originally a Scandinavian settlement, bypassed by the busy A.171 at the top of a long descent into Eskdale. It has two hotels, accommodation in private houses and large caravan sites along the cliff top overlooking the sea.

Hawsker

Walkers who now really have the bit between their teeth will spurn the opportunity of an overnight stay in Hawsker. The road signposted Robin Hood's Bay 2½ miles, carrying a bus service, is taken until it curves to the right, when faithful followers of the route continue ahead down a lane, passing a caravan site and then crossing the track of a former railway to the Bay. The latter, incidentally, offers a good fast walk to the Bay but like the tarmac road and the bus service, is a soft option to be resisted. Such reluctance to take the quickest ways to the destination is rather like a cat playing with a mouse before administering the coup de grâce, but the fact is that the royal road to the Bay undoubtedly is along the cliff path, pouncing on the prey from a height. So the route continues past another caravan site and within minutes provides the sight long and eagerly awaited – the towering coastal cliffs and the limitless expanse of the North Sea beyond. A great moment, a fine reward for many days of effort.

Excitement is now at fever pitch as gulls scream a raucous welcome. Here is the cliff path that ends in the streets of Robin Hood's Bay (and, incidentally, is used also by the long-distance Cleveland Way). Here is the lofty headland above Maw Wyke Hole as a prelude to a magnificent high-level traverse with many dramatic glimpses of waves pounding the rocks below. This final section is a counterpart to the first – an exhilarating three-mile walk along the edge of cliffs, but this time with spirits uplifted by the realisation that nothing can now happen to prevent a successful ending, that within an hour it will be finished. The path, accompanied by walls and fences to stop encroachment into danger, needs no further written description, and here Derry can take over with his camera and give an impression in pictures of the coastal scenery along the way.

Maw Wyke Hole   Opposite *Sea cliffs near Robin Hood's Bay*

Opposite *Sea cliffs near Robin Hood's Bay*

Robin Hood's Bay

At last the massive headland of Ness Point is rounded and – a great moment, this – Robin Hood's Bay comes suddenly into view ahead as a sweeping curve rimmed by cliffs. The stiles on the path, some of them a sore trial for tired limbs, are succeeded by kissing gates, hinting that civilisation is near, and then, sure enough, a haphazard huddle of red roofs appears below at the one place where the cliffs relent to admit a stony beach.

Baytown, the village of Robin Hood's Bay   Opposite *Baytown*

With flags flying, the adrenalin flowing fiercely, and enjoying an acute personal satisfaction, the descent commences, passing a coastguard station and then an avenue of modern villas typical of suburbia anywhere, especially with its name of Mount Pleasant North. The older and more picturesque part of the village, properly called Baytown but far better known as Robin Hood's Bay, is entered down a flight of steps leading into a maze of narrow streets reserved for pedestrian use. Up the steep hill, in another suburbia, buses for Whitby and Scarborough are waiting, but they must wait a little longer until a ritual has been observed. The cramped streets and alleyways are invariably congested with visitors, today unaware that a great feat is about to be accomplished and in any case not caring a damn that a hero has joined their ranks. In fact, a man with a pack on his back feels uncomfortable and rather lonely, in the midst of the throng of visitors; his travel-stained outfit and heavy boots seem out of place among the smart clothes and sandals of those around him. No matter: clothes don't make a man, and a Coast to Coast walker arriving here has every right to consider himself a man above other men; after all, few of these happy holiday-makers could do or would have the initiative and courage to do what he has just done – 190 miles on foot!

Journey's end   Opposite *The shore, Robin Hood's Bay*

So with head held high, the Coast to Coast walker completes the journey from one side of England to the other by going down the streets to the slipway, passing the Baytown Hotel, where in a few minutes a very private celebration will take place, and finally, to the astonishment of lounging onlookers, strides out across the beach until his boots are lapped by the North Sea.

INDEX OF PLACES ON THE ROUTE

ALFRED WAINWRIGHT was born in Blackburn in 1907 and started work as an office boy in the local town hall at the age of thirteen. He moved to Kendal in 1941, becoming Borough Treasurer in 1948. His seven guidebooks to the Lakeland Fells were compiled between 1952 and 1966 and for this labour of love, as he calls it, he was awarded the MBE. His *Pennine Way Companion* followed in 1968. Since retiring, he has prepared over forty other guidebooks and volumes of drawings. Also with Derry Brabbs, he has written *Fellwalking with Wainwright* and *Wainwright on the Pennine Way*.

FELLWALKING WITH WAINWRIGHT

'Wainwright's pithy, humorous style is so full of passion for the Lakeland Fells that he has been mentioned in the same breath as Wordsworth and Coleridge by people discussing the literary greats of the area. Hardened rock climbers get lumps in their throats at some of his writings about the mountain tops.' *Sunday Times*

'. . . a joyous, almost celebratory, guided tour of eighteen of the author's favourite Lake District walks.' *Yorkshire Post*

'. . . the ideal guide by the most knowledgeable Northern walker, cartographer and climbing enthusiast of our time. The book is typical of Alfred Wainwright's thoroughness: each walk is described in detail, augmented by route maps and diagrams. The photographs by Derry Brabbs not only add colourful and graphic point to the instructions, but are works of rare beauty in themselves.' *House and Garden*

WAINWRIGHT ON THE PENNINE WAY

'A living legend . . . Every time Mr Wainwright stops and looks he has something to say that makes you want to stop and listen . . . Mr Wainwright's style is perfectly matched by Derry Brabb's lingeringly evocative camera.' *Sunday Telegraph*

'Once again with quite extraordinarily good colour photographs by Derry Brabbs, the author describes the 270-mile Pennine Way walk in his inimitable, infectious manner.' *Good Book Guide*